Pythagoras and Trigonometry

By Robert Watchman

An Easy Steps Math series book

Copyright © 2016 Robert Watchman

All rights reserved.

No portion of this publication may be reproduced, transmitted or broadcast in whole or in part or in any way without the written permission of the author.

Books in the Easy Steps Math series

Fractions
Decimals
Percentages
Ratios
Negative Numbers
Algebra
Pythogoras' Theorem and Trigonometry
Master Collection 1 – Fractions, Decimals and Percentages
Master Collection 2 – Fractions, Decimals and Ratios
Master Collection 3 – Fractions, Percentages and Ratios
Master Collection 4 – Decimals, Percentages and Ratios

More to Follow

Contents

Introduction	7
Chapter 1 **Pythagoras' Theorem Basics**	9
Chapter 2 **Surds**	11
Chapter 3 **Right Triangles or Right Angled Triangles**	20
Chapter 4 **Pythagoras' Theorem**	21
Chapter 5 **Pythagorean Triples or Pythagorean Triplets**	31
Chapter 6 **Applications of Pythagoras' Theorem**	32
Chapter 7 **Trigonometry Basics**	34
Chapter 8 **Trigonometric (Trig) Ratios**	41
Chapter 9 **Finding the Side Lengths of Right Triangles**	52
Chapter 10 **Finding the Value of Angles**	63
Chapter 11 **Angles of Elevation and Depression**	69
Chapter 12 **Bearings**	74
Chapter 13 **The Law of Sines (Sine Rule)**	86
Chapter 14 **The law of Cosines 9Cosine Rule)**	91
Chapter 15 **Mixed Application Questions**	99
Multiplication Tables	101
Answers	104
Glossary of Useful Terms	107

Introduction

This series of books has been written for the purpose of simplifying mathematical concepts that many students (and parents) find difficult. The explanations in many textbooks and on the Internet are often confusing and bogged down with terminology. This book has been written in a step-by-step 'verbal' style, meaning, the instructions are what would be said to students in class to explain the concepts in an easy to understand way.

Students are taught how to do their work in class, but when they get home, many do not necessarily recall how to answer the questions they learned about earlier that day. All they see are numbers in their books with no easy-to-follow explanation of what to do. This is a very common problem, especially when new concepts are being taught.

For over twenty years I have been writing math notes on the board for students to copy into a note book (separate from their work book), so when they go home they will still know how the questions are supposed to be answered. The excuse of not understanding or forgetting how to do the work is becoming a thing of the past. Many students have commented that when they read over these notes, either for completing homework or studying for a test or exam, they hear my voice going through the explanations again.

Once students start seeing success, they start to enjoy math rather than dread it. Students have found much success in using the notes from class to aid them in their study. In fact students from other classes have been seen using photocopies of the notes given in my classes. In one instance a parent found my math notes so easy to follow that he copied them to use in teaching his students in his school.

You will find this step-by-step method of learning easier to follow than traditional styles of explanation. With questions included throughout, you will gain practice along with a newfound understanding of how to complete your calculations. Answers are included at the end.

Chapter 1

Pythagoras' Theorem Basics

Pythagoras' theorem is a rule which identifies the relationship among the three side lengths of a right triangle.
The difficulty with Pythagoras' theorem isn't in applying the formula, the formula is easy $c^2 = a^2 + b^2$, instead the difficulty is in dealing with squares, square roots, cubes, cubed roots, surds, rational and irrational numbers, right triangles (or right-angled triangles), etc. To be successful with Pythagoras, these concepts and ideas will need to be learned. Below are some explanations of these terms. These explanations are enough to make sure you can properly answer the required questions for Pythagoras' theorem. Further explanations would be too much for this book and will come in future books.

Rational and Irrational Numbers

Rational numbers are the numbers that **can** easily be written as fractions or ratios.
E.g.

2 is a rational number because it can be written as $\frac{2}{1}$.

1.56 is a rational number because it can be written as $\frac{156}{100}$ or $1\frac{56}{100}$ or simplified down to $1\frac{14}{25}$.

0.0001 is a rational number because it can be written as $\frac{1}{10000}$.

Irrational numbers are the numbers that <u>cannot</u> be written as fractions or ratios as they have too many decimal places, and they **do not** have a repeating pattern.

E.g. $\sqrt{2}$ is an irrational number because it cannot be written as a simple fraction or ratio and it doesn't have a repeating pattern. In fact, the first 15 decimal places of $\sqrt{2}$ is 1.414213562373095, and it goes on for quite a bit longer. If you want to see $\sqrt{2}$ to one million decimal places, NASA has a cool site for this. Go to:

http://apod.nasa.gov/htmltest/gifcity/sqrt2.1mil

$\sqrt{3}$ is the same, so is $\sqrt{5}$, $\sqrt{7}$ and more.
So when dealing with these types of numbers, they can be left as they are rather than be converted to decimals. $\sqrt{2}$ is much easier to work with than 1.414213562373095….
These irrational numbers, which are written with square root signs ($\sqrt{}$), are called <u>surds</u>.

Chapter 2

Surds

A surd is a number that has been left with a square root sign ($\sqrt{}$). As mentioned above, surds are irrational numbers. The advantage of leaving a number as a surd is that the surd is an <u>exact value</u>. This means that $\sqrt{2}$ is exact whereas 1.414213562373095… is an approximation and harder to work with. Of course if a question says **'give your answer correct to 2 decimal places'**, then you must use the decimal value, but if the question asks for an exact value then $\sqrt{2}$, or $\sqrt{5}$, or $\sqrt{11}$, etc is what you would write. Don't forget, answers must always be simplified.

There are certain rules that can help make calculating and simplifying surds easier.

Rule 1. $\sqrt{a \times b} = \sqrt{a} \times \sqrt{b}$

E.g. Simplify $\sqrt{27}$.

Separate the number into 2 factors as shown. One of the factors **must** be a perfect square.

$\sqrt{27} = \sqrt{9 \times 3}$

Each of the factors can now be written with its own square root sign.

$= \sqrt{9} \times \sqrt{3}$

As the 9 is a perfect square, it can be rewritten as a square number.

$= \sqrt{3^2} \times \sqrt{3}$

The factor that is a perfect square can be simplified to a whole number. So **the square root of 3 squared is 3**. (This idea applies to all numbers and algebra also i.e. $\sqrt{12^2} = 12$, $\sqrt{c^2} = c$, etc.).

$= 3 \times \sqrt{3}$

The answer can be written without the multiplications sign.

$= 3\sqrt{3}$

In this instance, 27 can be changed to 9 x 3, and the square root of 9 is 3. The important part of this exercise is that one of the factors of the surd must be a **'perfect square'**, that is a number whose square root is a whole number. In the above example, 9 is a perfect square because the square root of 9 is 3.

Here is another example.

Simplify $\sqrt{50}$

$\sqrt{50} = \sqrt{25 \times 2}$

$= \sqrt{25} \times \sqrt{2}$

$= \sqrt{5^2} \times \sqrt{2}$

$= 5 \times \sqrt{2}$

$= 5\sqrt{2}$

Don't forget that when there are two surds, they can also be multiplied to make one surd. This is the reverse of what was done above.

I.e. $\sqrt{a} \times \sqrt{b} = \sqrt{a \times b}$

E.g. $\sqrt{2} \times \sqrt{5}$

$= \sqrt{2 \times 5}$

$= \sqrt{10}$

Rule 2. $\sqrt{\dfrac{a}{b}} = \dfrac{\sqrt{a}}{\sqrt{b}}$

E.g. Simplify $\sqrt{\dfrac{108}{162}}$

A single square root sign can be split into two, one over the numerator and one over the denominator.

$$\sqrt{\dfrac{108}{162}} = \dfrac{\sqrt{108}}{\sqrt{162}}$$

Now follow rule 1 for the top and bottom.

$$= \dfrac{\sqrt{36 \times 3}}{\sqrt{81 \times 2}}$$

$$= \dfrac{\sqrt{36} \times \sqrt{3}}{\sqrt{81} \times \sqrt{2}}$$

$$= \dfrac{6 \times \sqrt{3}}{9 \times \sqrt{2}}$$

Simplify the fraction by working out what number goes into the numerator and denominator. In this case it's 3.
3 goes into 6 twice and into 9 three times. (See Easy Steps Math Fractions if you don't know how to do this.)

$$= \dfrac{^2\cancel{6} \times \sqrt{3}}{^3\cancel{9} \times \sqrt{2}}$$

And the final answer is

$$= \frac{2\sqrt{3}}{3\sqrt{2}}$$

Again, don't forget that surds that are being divided should be simplified as far as possible.

I.e. $\dfrac{\sqrt{a}}{\sqrt{b}} = \sqrt{\dfrac{a}{b}}$

E.g. $\dfrac{\sqrt{30}}{\sqrt{6}} = \sqrt{\dfrac{30}{6}}$

$= \sqrt{5}$

Rule 3. $a\sqrt{b} + c\sqrt{b} = (a+c)\sqrt{b}$ or $a\sqrt{b} - c\sqrt{b} = (a-c)\sqrt{b}$

This uses the distributive law (see Easy Steps Math Algebra).

E.g. Evaluate $3\sqrt{5} + 7\sqrt{5}$

$3\sqrt{5} + 7\sqrt{5} = (3+7)\sqrt{5}$ This can only be done if the numbers under the square root sign are the same, in this case 5.

$= 10\sqrt{5}$ The 3 and the 7 can be added.

The same rule applies for subtraction.
Evaluate $9\sqrt{7} - 7\sqrt{7}$

$9\sqrt{7} - 7\sqrt{7} = (9-7)\sqrt{7}$

$= 2\sqrt{7}$

Rule 4. $\dfrac{a}{\sqrt{b}} = \dfrac{a}{\sqrt{b}} \times \dfrac{\sqrt{b}}{\sqrt{b}}$

E.g. Rationalise the denominator of $\dfrac{7}{\sqrt{3}}$

Since the denominator of the fraction is an irrational number, it is best if it is converted to a rational number. We do this by using the irrational denominator to create another fraction as shown, but since this other fraction equals 1 the value of the original fraction won't change (see Easy Steps Math Fractions); it will just look different. Now multiply these two fractions.

$$\dfrac{7}{\sqrt{3}} = \dfrac{7}{\sqrt{3}} \times \dfrac{\sqrt{3}}{\sqrt{3}}$$

$$= \dfrac{7 \times \sqrt{3}}{\sqrt{3} \times \sqrt{3}}$$

Since $\sqrt{3} \times \sqrt{3} = 3$ the denominator now has a rational number.

$$= \dfrac{7\sqrt{3}}{3}$$

Rule 5. $\dfrac{a}{b+\sqrt{d}} = \dfrac{a}{b+\sqrt{d}} \times \dfrac{b-\sqrt{d}}{b-\sqrt{d}}$

E.g. Rationalise the denominator of $\dfrac{\sqrt{2}}{\sqrt{11}+3}$

Again, since the denominator of the fraction is irrational it is best if it is converted to a rational number. We do this by using the irrational denominator to create another fraction as shown, but again, since this fraction equals 1 the value of the original fraction won't change; it will just look different. Note however, that in this situation, the fraction equalling 1, the plus (+) sign must be changed to a minus (-) sign, top and bottom.

$$\frac{\sqrt{2}}{\sqrt{11}+3} = \frac{\sqrt{2}}{\sqrt{11}+3} \times \frac{\sqrt{11}-3}{\sqrt{11}-3}$$

The next step requires the use of the distributive law to multiply both the top and bottom. Note the denominator will use the D.O.T.S method of expansion (see Easy Steps Math Algebra). Now expand the brackets top and bottom.

$$= \frac{\sqrt{2}(\sqrt{11}-3)}{(\sqrt{11}+3)(\sqrt{11}-3)}$$

$$= \frac{\sqrt{2} \times \sqrt{11} - \sqrt{2} \times 3}{11 - 3\sqrt{11} + 3\sqrt{11} - 9}$$

Complete the calculations in the numerator and denominator to get...

$$= \frac{\sqrt{22} - 3\sqrt{2}}{11-9}$$

This is the final answer

$$= \frac{\sqrt{22} - 3\sqrt{2}}{2}$$

Rule 6. $\dfrac{a}{b-\sqrt{d}} = \dfrac{a}{b-\sqrt{d}} \times \dfrac{b+\sqrt{d}}{b+\sqrt{d}}$ This is the same as **Rule 5**, but with the opposite signs.

E.g. Rationalise the denominator of $\dfrac{\sqrt{2}}{\sqrt{11}-3}$

Once again, since the denominator of the fraction is irrational it is best if it is converted to a rational number. We do this by using the irrational denominator to create another fraction as shown, but again, since this fraction equals 1 the value of the original fraction won't change; it will just look different. Note however, that in this situation the fraction equalling 1, the minus (-) sign must be changed to a plus (+) sign, top and bottom.

$$\dfrac{\sqrt{2}}{\sqrt{11}-3} = \dfrac{\sqrt{2}}{\sqrt{11}-3} \times \dfrac{\sqrt{11}+3}{\sqrt{11}+3}$$

The next step requires the use of the distributive law to multiply both the top and bottom. Note the denominator will use the D.O.T.S method of expansion (see Easy Steps Math Algebra). Now expand the brackets top and bottom.

$$= \dfrac{\sqrt{2}(\sqrt{11}+3)}{(\sqrt{11}-3)(\sqrt{11}+3)}$$

$$= \dfrac{\sqrt{2} \times \sqrt{11} + \sqrt{2} \times 3}{11 + 3\sqrt{11} - 3\sqrt{11} - 9}$$

Complete the calculations in the numerator and denominator to get…

$$= \dfrac{\sqrt{22} + 3\sqrt{2}}{11 - 9}$$

This is the final answer.

$$= \frac{\sqrt{22}+3\sqrt{2}}{2}$$

*Note that surds can only be added or subtracted if the number under the square root signs are the same.

I.e.

$$a\sqrt{c}+b\sqrt{c}=(a+b)\sqrt{c} \text{ and } a\sqrt{c}-b\sqrt{c}=(a-b)\sqrt{c}$$

E.g. $3\sqrt{5}+4\sqrt{5}=(3+4)\sqrt{5}$

$$=7\sqrt{5}$$

Sometimes before adding or subtracting, the surds will need to be simplified.

$$7\sqrt{18}-3\sqrt{50}=7\sqrt{9\times 2}-3\sqrt{25\times 2}$$

$$=7\times 3\sqrt{2}-3\times 5\sqrt{2}$$

$$=21\sqrt{2}-15\sqrt{2}$$

$$=(21-15)\sqrt{2}$$

$$=6\sqrt{2}$$

Complete the following questions

Simplify these surds without a calculator

a) $\sqrt{32}$

b) $3\sqrt{27}$

c) $\dfrac{\sqrt{125}}{\sqrt{45}}$

d) $\dfrac{5\sqrt{49}}{7}$

e) $\sqrt{150} + 3\sqrt{54} - 4\sqrt{24}$

Rationalise the denominator of the following

f) $\dfrac{1}{\sqrt{2}}$

h) $\dfrac{1}{4+\sqrt{2}}$

g) $\dfrac{5}{\sqrt{8}}$

i) $\dfrac{\sqrt{5}}{\sqrt{3}-\sqrt{2}}$

Chapter 3

Right Triangles or Right Angled Triangles

The first two things to remember about a triangle are that it has three (3) sides and that the three angles inside the triangle must add up to $180°$.

In a right triangle, one of the angles is $90°$. This is called the **right angle** and is symbolized with a small square in one of the corners, as shown below.

E.g.

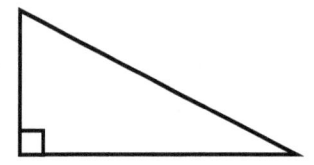

This small square is important because it shows that this particular angle is $90°$. If this square were not drawn in, it would have to assume the triangle is not a right triangle.

Now since the right angle is $90°$ then the remaining two angles can only add up to $90°$. Therefore the total of the angles is $180°$.

This information becomes more important when we are looking at Trigonometry in the second part of this book. The important point here is that Pythagoras' theorem is used with right triangles.

The **Hypotenuse** of a right triangle is the longest side of the triangle. There is only one long side on a right triangle and to find this long side, you can draw a line through two of the corners of the square and it will point to the hypotenuse.

E.g.

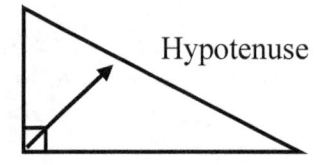

Hypotenuse

Chapter 4

Pythagoras' Theorem

Pythagoras' theorem states that **'the square of the hypotenuse is equal to the sum of the other two sides squared.'**

This means that the area of the box where c is, is equal to the area of the box where a is plus the area of the box where b is. (the a box plus the b box equals the c box).

Visually this theorem looks like this, with the hypotenuse labelled c and the other two sides labelled a and b:

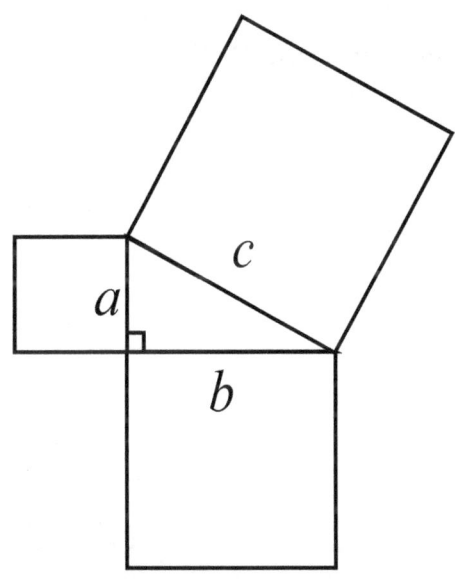

So Pythagoras' theorem is $c^2 = a^2 + b^2$. This formula allows us to find the length of any side of a right triangle if we know the lengths of the other two sides.

E.g. The right triangle below has the side lengths as shown.

Find the length of the hypotenuse c.

```
     c
3 ⌐────
    4
```

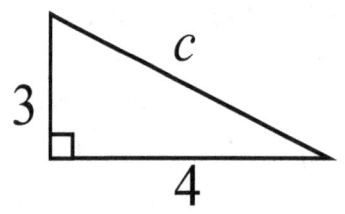

Using Pythagoras' Formula:
Always start with the formula
$$c^2 = a^2 + b^2$$

Substitute in the values that are known. In this case a and b
$$c^2 = 3^2 + 4^2$$

Now do the necessary calculations
$$c^2 = 9 + 16$$

$$c^2 = 25$$
Now find the value of c.
$$\sqrt{c^2} = \sqrt{25}$$

$$c = 5$$.

Sometimes the formula $c^2 = a^2 + b^2$ can be rewritten as

$$c = \sqrt{a^2 + b^2}$$

Substitute in the numbers for a and b and complete the calculations

$$c = \sqrt{3^2 + 4^2}$$

$$c = \sqrt{9+16}$$

$$c = \sqrt{25}$$

$$c = 5$$

Sometimes it is one of the the other two sides of the triangle which is unknown.
E.g. i)

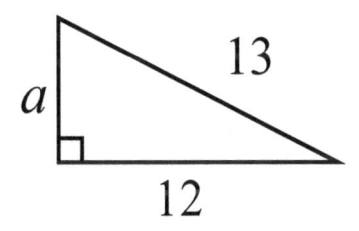

or ii)

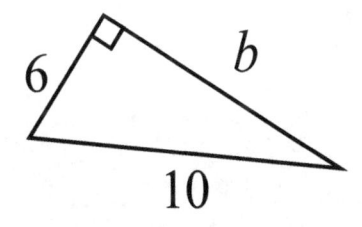

In these situations, the formula used can be rearranged to work out each of the other two sides.

So,
$$c^2 = a^2 + b^2$$ is rearranged to $$a^2 = c^2 - b^2$$ to find the value of a or to $$b^2 = c^2 - a^2$$ to find the value of b.

Remember these can also be written as $a = \sqrt{c^2 - b^2}$ and $b = \sqrt{c^2 - a^2}$.

E.g. Using the examples above:

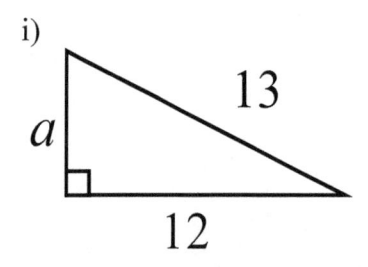

i)

Right triangle with hypotenuse 13, base 12, and vertical side a.

Start with the formula,
$$a^2 = c^2 - b^2$$
Substitute in the values that are known,
$$a^2 = 13^2 - 12^2$$
Do the necessary calculations,
$$a^2 = 169 - 144$$
$$a^2 = 25$$

$a = \sqrt{25}$

$a = 5$

ii)

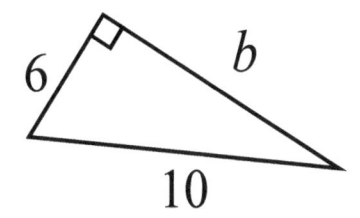

[Triangle with right angle, legs 6 and b, hypotenuse 10]

Start with the formula

$b^2 = c^2 - a^2$

Rearranging the formula,

$b = \sqrt{c^2 - a^2}$

Substitute in the values that are known,

$b = \sqrt{10^2 - 6^2}$

Do the necessary calculations

$b = \sqrt{100 - 36}$

$b = \sqrt{64}$

$b = 8$

Now complete the following questions.

Use Pythagoras' Theorem to find the value of the unknown side.
Give exact answers or correct to 2 decimal places if required.

a)

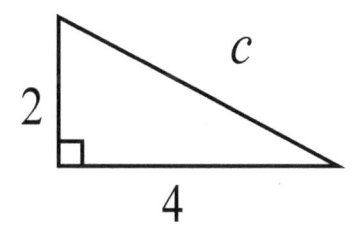

2

4

c

b)

c

6

8

c)

12

5

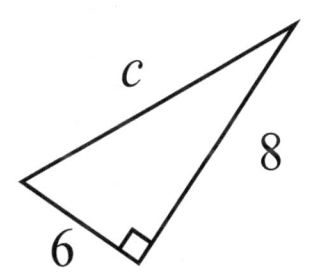

c

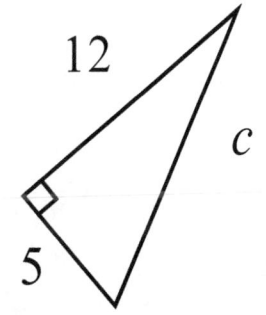

d)

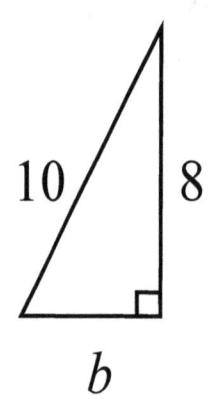

Triangle with legs 8 and b, hypotenuse 10.

e)

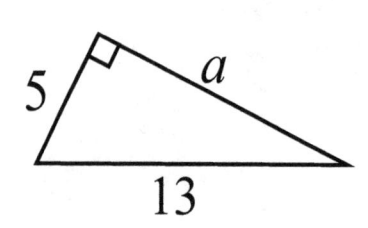

Right triangle with legs 5 and a, hypotenuse 13.

f)

Right triangle with legs 6 and 5, hypotenuse a.

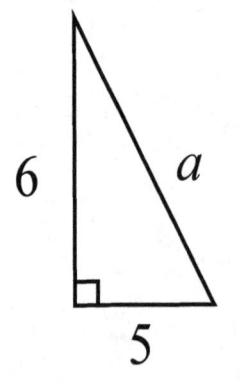

g) Give answers correct to 2 decimal places.

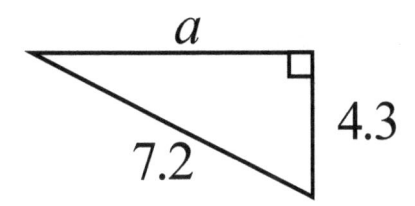

h)

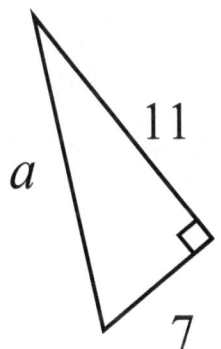

i)

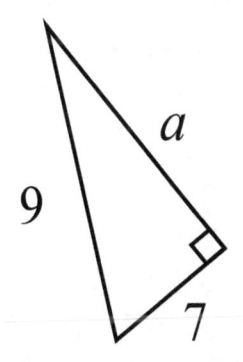

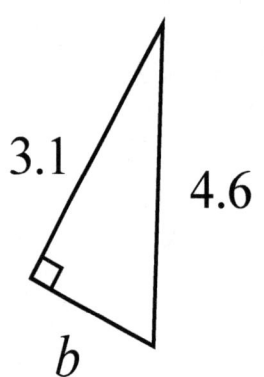

j)

3.1 4.6

b

Chapter 5

Pythagorean Triples or Pythagorean Triplets

One of the examples above demonstrates that a right triangle with side lengths of 3 and 4 will have a hypotenuse of 5. If the side lengths are 5 and 12, the hypotenuse will be 13. If the side lengths are 8 and 15, the hypotenuse will be 17. Again, if the side lengths are 7 and 24, the hypotenuse will be 25. These are common numbers that make up right triangles. Conversely if a triangles have values of 3,4,5 or 5,12,13 or 8,15,17 or 7,24,25 for the three side lengths, then the triangle will be a right triangle. These sets of three numbers are examples of **Pythagorean Triples**.Of course these are not the only numbers that make up these triples, but they are easy ones to remember.
The multiples of these sets of numbers are also Pythagorean Triples. For instance, if the numbers 3,4,5 are multiplied by 2 the result will be 6,8,10. If they are multiplied by 3, the result will be 9,12,15, etc. The rule applies to all of these and to all Pythagorean Triples. Wikipedia Encyclopedia gives more examples of these triples.

Chapter 6

Applications of Pythagoras' Theorem

As interesting as Pythagoras' Theorem is, the main purpose for it is to help solve problems. The idea behind solving the problem is to, of course, find the right triangle first.

E.g. A support wire is attached to a flagpole 8m above ground level. If the other end is attached to the ground 6m from the base of the pole, how long does the wire need to be?

Step 1: Draw the diagram of the situation and label the known lengths.

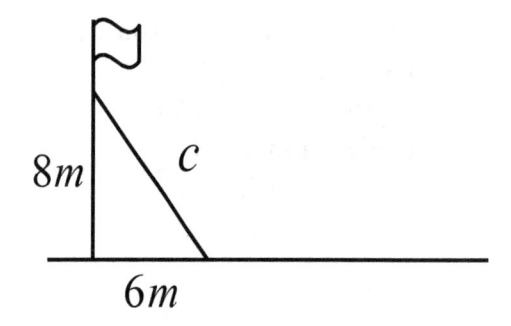

8m

c

6m

Step 2: Identify the right triangle from the diagram

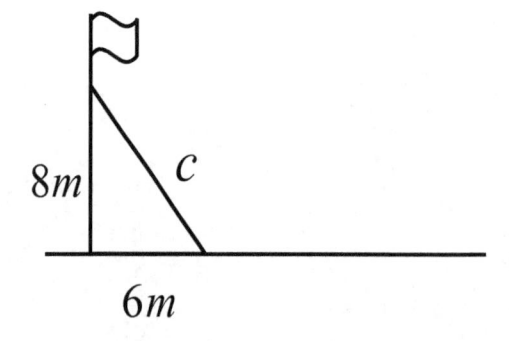

8m

c

6m

Step 3: Use Pythagoras' theorem to find the length of c.
As the values 6 and 8 make up a Pythagorean Triple, the length of the wire will be 10m.

There are many many other application type questions which can be solved using Pythagoras' Theorem. The important part is to identify the right triangle first, and then apply the formula.

Chapter 7

Trigonometry Basics

Trigonometry is the study of the relationship between the angles and the side lengths of right triangles. These relationships aid in the formation of **trigonometric (trig) ratios** which are used to help solve problems which include side lengths and angles of right triangles. Therefore trigonometry is used to find the value of unknown angles inside a right triangle, as ell as finding the lengths of the sides.

In order to better learn the ratios, each side of the right triangle must be identified.

The Hypotenuse
The **hypotenuse** is the same for all right triangles. It is the longest of the three sides. (see Pythagoras' Theorem above) The other two sides are called the Opposite side and the Adjacent side. The angle used when working with these three sides is usually called **Theta** and it's symbol is θ. Theta (θ) is used when the value of the angle is not known. If the value of the angle is known, this will be used instead of θ. This however, does not change any of the rules that follow. Note that Theta can be replaced with any other variable.

The Adjacent Side
The word **adjacent** means 'next to'. So the adjacent side is **always** going to be next to the angle θ. Of course this means the angle will be **between** the hypotenuse and the adjacent side.

E.g.

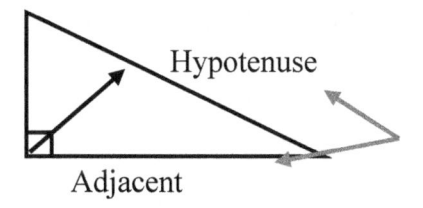

[Triangle diagram labeled "Hypotenuse" and "Adjacent"]

Note that the angle is between the hypotenuse and the adjacent side.

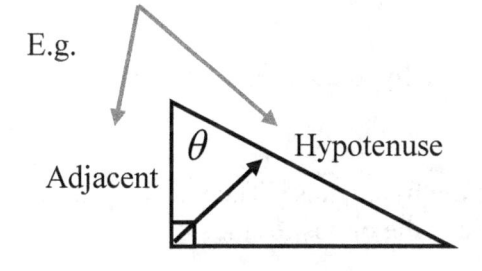

Now the important thing to remember here is that if the position of the angle θ changes, the adjacent side will also change. Theta (θ) must always stay between the hypotenuse and the adjacent side. So in the example above if θ was in the other corner, then the adjacent side would move also.

Again the angle is between the hypotenuse and the adjacent side

E.g.

[Triangle diagram labeled "Adjacent", "θ", and "Hypotenuse"]

The Opposite Side

The third side of the triangle is the **opposite** side and its position will depend on where the adjacent side is. So in our two triangles above, the three sides will look like this:

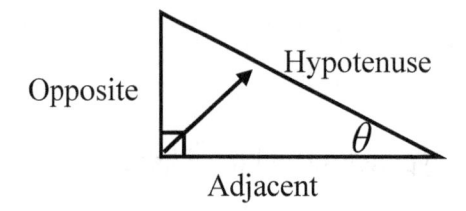

Triangle with Opposite (vertical left side), Hypotenuse (slanted top, with arrow), Adjacent (bottom), and angle θ at the bottom right.

or, if the angle θ changes,

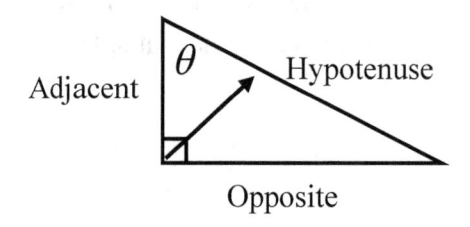

Triangle with Adjacent (vertical left side), Hypotenuse (slanted top, with arrow), Opposite (bottom), and angle θ at the top left.

Note that the angle is never between the hypotenuse and the opposite side.

To recap, the longest side is always the hypotenuse. The side next to θ is the adjacent side and the third side is the opposite side.

The arrow pointing to the hypotenuse is not part of the calculation. It is only there to show how to find the hypotenuse.

When answering a question in trigonometry, it is easiest to identify the three sides in the order mentioned above. That is, identify the hypotenuse first and write **H** next to it, then look for the angle θ and write **A** for adjacent next to that side. The third side is the opposite side, so put **O** next to it. Always follow this order to help reduce mistakes.

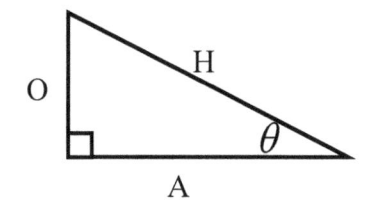

Complete the following questions.

In each of the following triangles, identify whether the x represents the adjacent, hypotenuse or opposite sides.

a)

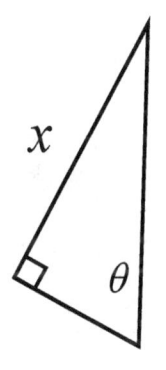

b)

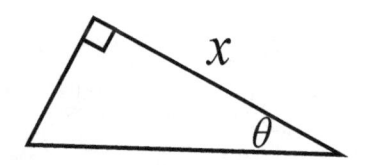

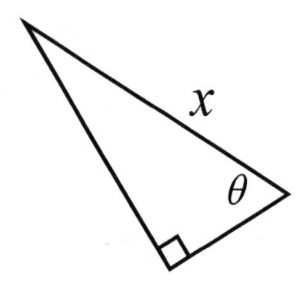

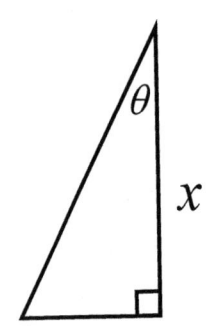

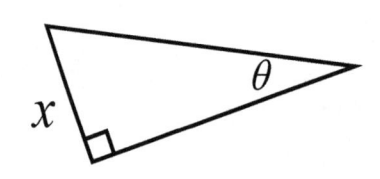

c)

d)

e)

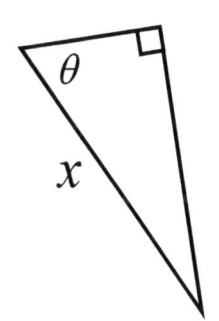

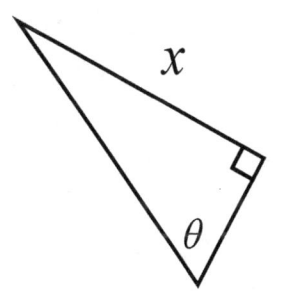

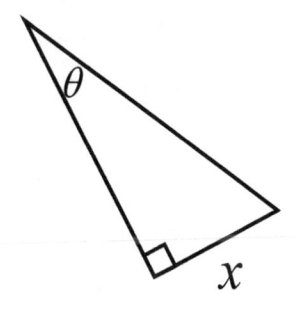

f)

g)

h)

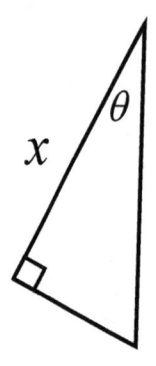

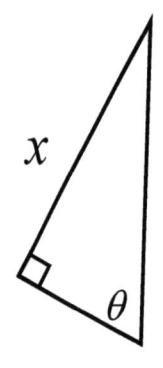

i)

j)

Chapter 8

Trigonometric (Trig) Ratios

There are three basic trigonometric ratios, these are **sine**, **cosine** and **tangent**, abbreviated to **'sin'**, **'cos'** and **'tan'**. A scientific calculator will be required for this topic and it must have the basic trigonometric functions available.

These ratios use one angle and two of the three sides of a triangle, mentioned above, to help with calculations.

The ratios are:

$$\sin\theta = \frac{opposite}{hypotenuse}$$

$$\cos\theta = \frac{adjacent}{hypotenuse}$$

$$\tan\theta = \frac{opposite}{adjacent}$$

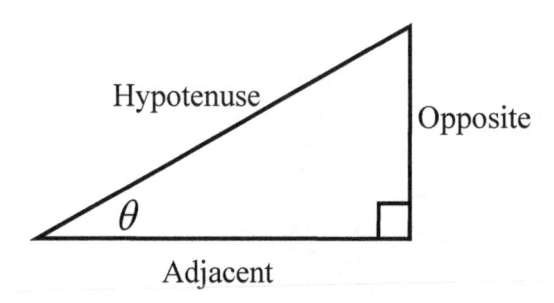

As a shortcut, these ratios can be written as:

$$S = \frac{O}{H}, \; C = \frac{A}{H}, \text{ and } T = \frac{O}{A}.$$

Taking each of the letters above and putting them together forms *SOH CAH TOA*. This 'expression' can be used to remember which ratio to use and when.

What all this information means is:

- to find the sine of the angle θ the length of the opposite side is put over the length of the hypotenuse,
    - to find the cosine of the angle θ the length of the adjacent side is put over the length of the hypotenuse, and
    - to find the tangent of the angle θ the length of the opposite side is put over the length of the adjacent side.

Conversely, if the lengths of the opposite side and the hypotenuse are given, the sine ratio will be used. If the lengths of the adjacent side and the hypotenuse are given, the cosine ratio will be used and if the lengths of the opposite side and the adjacent side are given, the tangent ratio will be used.

Try these questions

Which two sides of the triangles below would be used to calculate the given ratio.

a) $\sin \theta$

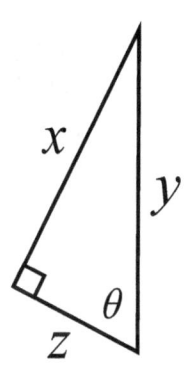

b) $\cos \theta$

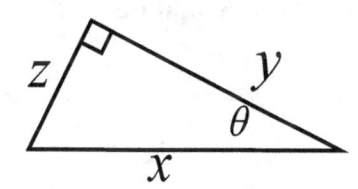

c) $\tan \theta$

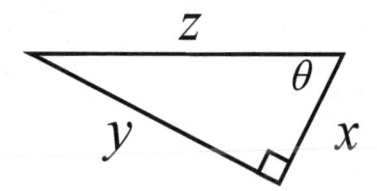

d) sin θ

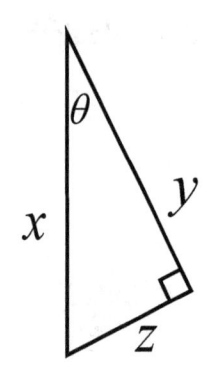

e) cos θ

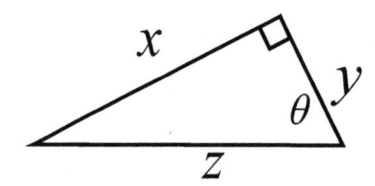

For each of the following, identify which trig ratio would be used.

f)

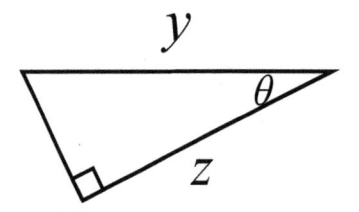

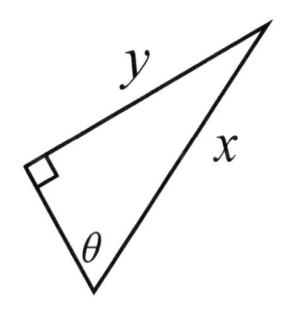

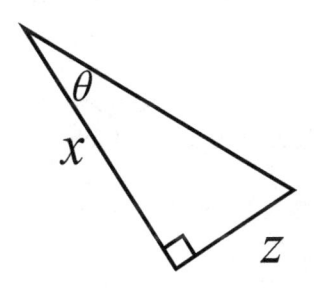

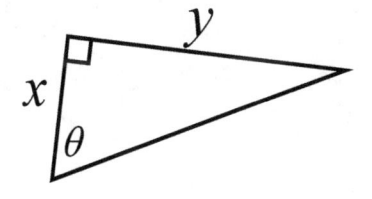

g)

h)

i)

j)

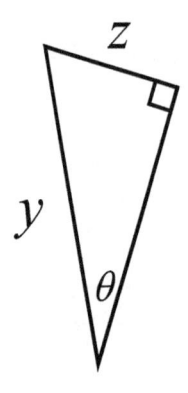

This method can be used to calculate the ratios of right triangles given specific side lengths.

E.g. In the three examples below, the same side values will be used, with each of the different ratios, to show the different results which would be obtained.

i) Find the value of sin θ.

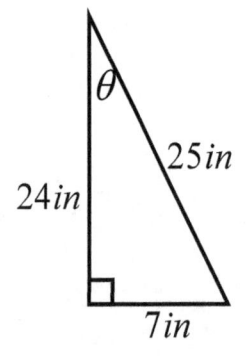

Step 1: Label the three sides of the triangle (i.e. O, H and A)

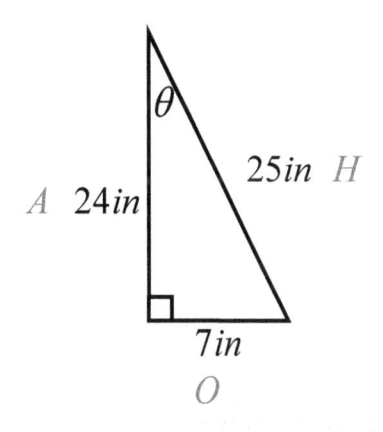

```
         θ
                  25in  H
A  24in

         7in
          O
```

Step 2: Start with the formula.

$$sin\theta = \frac{O}{H}$$

Step 3: Substitute in the known values.

In this case the opposite side is 7 and the hypotenuse is 25.

$$sin\theta = \frac{7}{25}$$

Therefore the answer is $\frac{7}{25}$ or 0.28 if converted to a decimal.

ii) Find the value of cos θ.

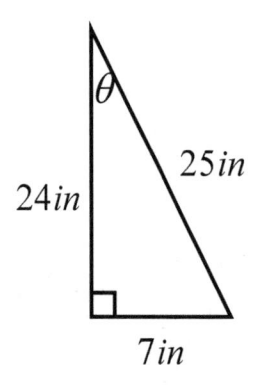

[Triangle with vertical side 24in (left), hypotenuse 25in, horizontal side 7in (bottom), angle θ at top]

Step 1: Label the three sides of the triangle (i.e. O, H and A)

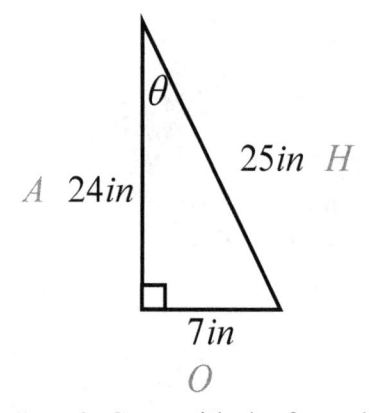

[Triangle with A 24in (left side), 25in H (hypotenuse), 7in O (bottom), angle θ at top]

Step 2: Start with the formula.

$$\cos\theta = \frac{A}{H}$$

Step 2: Substitute in the known values.

In this case the adjacent side is 24 and the hypotenuse is 25.

$$\cos\theta = \frac{24}{25}$$

Therefore the answer is $\frac{24}{25}$ or 0.96 if converted to a decimal.

iii) Find the value of tan θ.

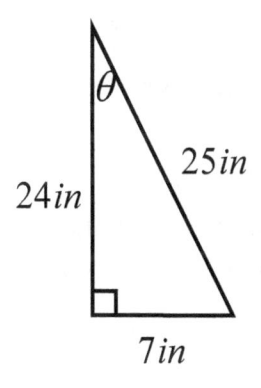

Step 1: Label the three sides of the triangle (i.e. O, H and A)

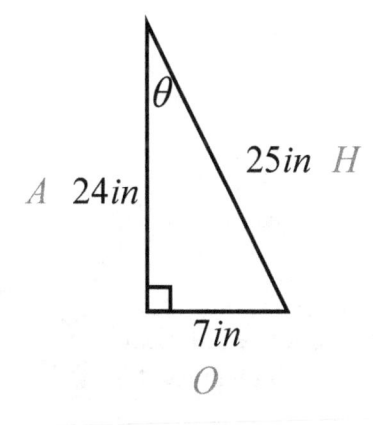

Step 2: Start with the formula.

$$tan\theta = \frac{O}{A}$$

Step 3: Substitute in the known values.

In this case the opposite side is 7 and the adjacent side is 24.

$$tan\theta = \frac{7}{24}$$

The answer is $\frac{7}{24}$ or 0.2917 if converted to a decimal, corrected to 4 decimal places.

Now as mentioned above, if θ was located in the other position the results would be different.

I.e.

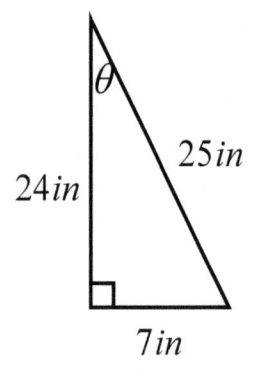

With θ in this new position, 24 becomes the opposite side and 7 becomes the adjacent side. The hypotenuse doesn't change. It is always the longest side of the triangle.

Therefore sin θ becomes $\frac{24}{25}$ or 0.96, cos θ becomes $\frac{7}{25}$ or 0.28, and tan θ becomes $\frac{24}{7}$ or 3.4286, corrected to 4 decimal places.

Chapter 9

Finding the Side Lengths of Right Triangles

Trigonometry is very useful in finding the length of an unknown side of a right triangle. This can be done when an angle and another side length are known.
Algebra will be used for the calculations.

In the following 3 examples, the unknown side will be one of the two shorter sides of the triangle.

E.g. 1.

Find the length of the unknown side in the triangle below.

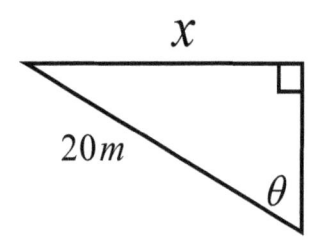

x

20m

θ

Step 1: Label the three sides of the triangle (i.e. O, H, and A).

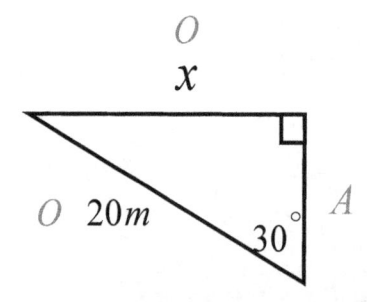

O
x

O 20m

A
30°

Since the relevant information is on the Opposite side and on the Hypotenuse, then the Sin ratio is to be used. (viz SOH CAH TOA).

Step 2: Start with the formula

$$sin\theta = \frac{O}{H}$$

Step 3: Substitute in the known information. In this case it is the value of the angle, 30° and the length of the hypotenuse, 20 m and the unknown value x.

$$sin30 = \frac{x}{20}$$

Step 4: Multiply both sides of the equals sign by 20. This is to make x the subject (See Easy Steps Math Algebra).

$$20 \times sin30 = \frac{x}{20} \times 20$$

this gives:

$$20 \times sin30 = x$$

Step 5: Input $20 \times sin30$ into a calculator.

And the answer will be 10 m. (Don't forget the units).

This same process is used for **cos.**

E.g. 2.

Find the length of the unknown side in the triangle below.

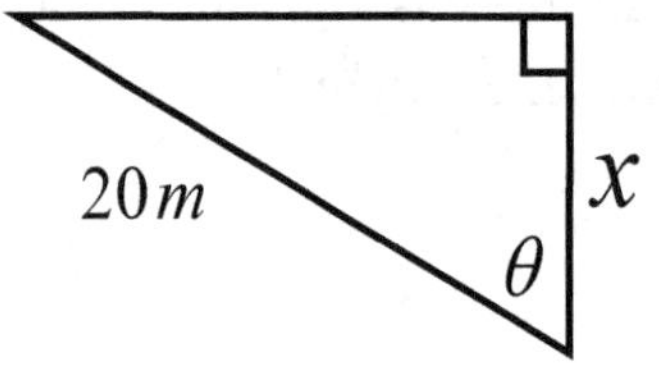

Step 1: Label the three sides of the triangle (i.e. O, H, and A).

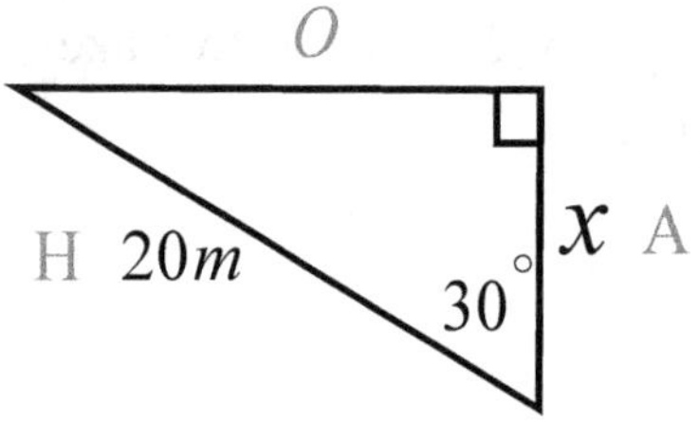

Since the relevant information is on the Adjacent side and on the Hypotenuse, then the cos ratio is to be used. (*SOH CAH TOA*)

Step 2: Start with the formula

$$cos\theta = \frac{A}{H}$$

Step 3: Substitute in the known information. In this case it is the value of the angle, 30° and the length of the hypotenuse, 20 m and the unknown value x.

$$cos30 = \frac{x}{20}$$

Step 4: Multiply both sides of the equals sign by 20. This is to make x the subject.

$$20 \times cos30 = \frac{x}{20} \times 20$$

this gives:

$$20 \times cos30 = x$$

Step 5: Input $20 \times cos30$ into a calculator,

And the answer will be 17.321 m.

And again the same process is used for **tan.**

E.g.3.

Find the length of the unknown side in the triangle below.

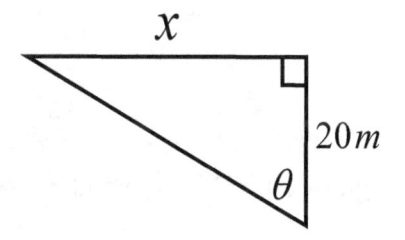

Step 1: Label the three sides of the triangle (i.e. O, H, and A).

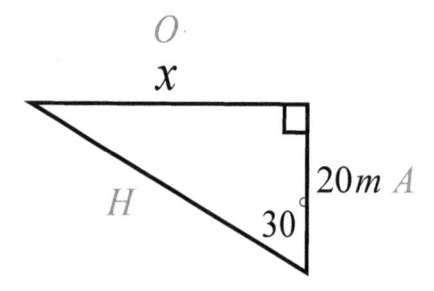

```
        O
        x
   H         │ 20m  A
       30°
```

Since the relevant information is on the Opposite side and on the Adjacent side, then the Tan ratio is to be used.
($SOH\ CAH\ TOA$)

Step 2: Start with the formula

$$tan\theta = \frac{O}{A}$$

Step 3: Substitute in the known information. In this case it is the value of the angle, 30° and the length of the adjacent side, 20 m and the unknown value x.

$$tan30 = \frac{x}{20}$$

Step 4: Multiply both sides of the equals sign by 20. This is to make x the subject.

$$20 \times tan30 = \frac{x}{20} \times 20$$

this gives:

$$20 \times tan30 = x$$

Step 5: Input $20 \times tan30$ into a calculator,

And the answer will be 11.547 m.

If the hypotenuse is the unknown side (for sin and cos), or the adjacent side is unknown (for tan), the procedure is the same, however an extra step in algebra is required.

E.g.4.
Find the length of the hypotenuse in the triangle below.

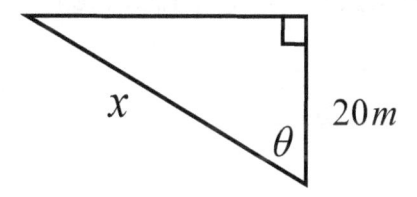

[Triangle diagram: right triangle with side x, side $20m$, angle θ]

Step 1: Label the three sides of the triangle (i.e. O, H, and A).

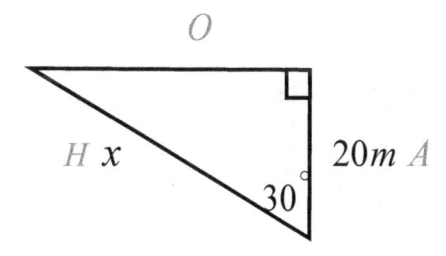

[Triangle diagram: labeled with O on top, H x on hypotenuse, $20m$ A on adjacent, angle $30°$]

Since the relevant information is on the Adjacent side and the Hypotenuse, then the Cos ratio is to be used. (SOH CAH TOA)

Step 2: Start with the formula

$$\cos\theta = \frac{A}{H}$$

Step 3: Substitute in the known information. In this case it is the value of the angle, 30°, the length of the Adjacent side, 20 m and the unknown value x.

$$\cos 30 = \frac{20}{x}$$

Note that when the hypotenuse needs to be found, the unknown value is on the denominator.

Step 4: Multiply both sides of the equals sign by x. (see Easy Steps Math Algebra)

$$x \times \cos 30 = \frac{20}{x} \times x$$

this gives:

$$x \times \cos 30 = 20$$

Step 5: Divide both sides of the equals sign by Cos 30

$$\frac{x \times \cos 30}{\cos 30} = \frac{20}{\cos 30}$$

this gives:

$$x = \frac{20}{\cos 30}$$

Step 6: Input $\frac{20}{\cos 30}$ this into a calculator,

And the answer will be 23.094 m. (Don't forget the units).

If the adjacent side needs to be found, and the ratio being used is Tan, the same procedure will be used to find the unknown side. This is because the value for the adjacent side will be on the denominator.

Try these questions

Find the length of the unknown side for these triangles. Give answers correct to two decimal places.

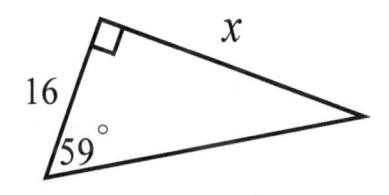

a)

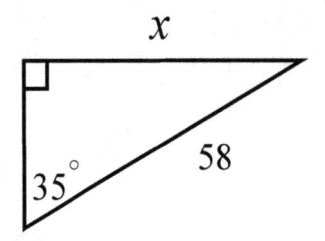

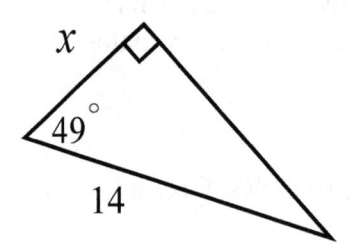

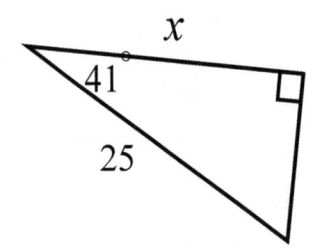

b)

x

58

35°

c)

x

49°

14

d)

x

41°

25

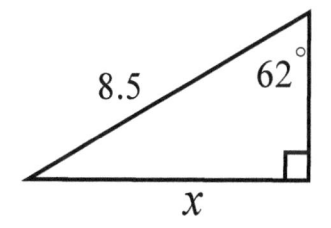

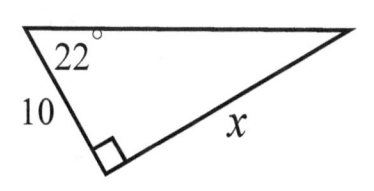

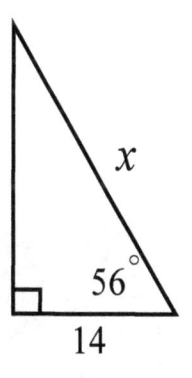

e)

8.5, 62°, x

f)

22°, 10, x

g)

x, 56°, 14

h)

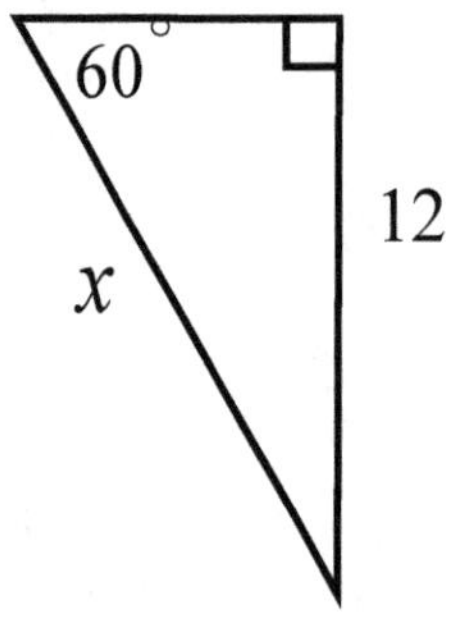

i)

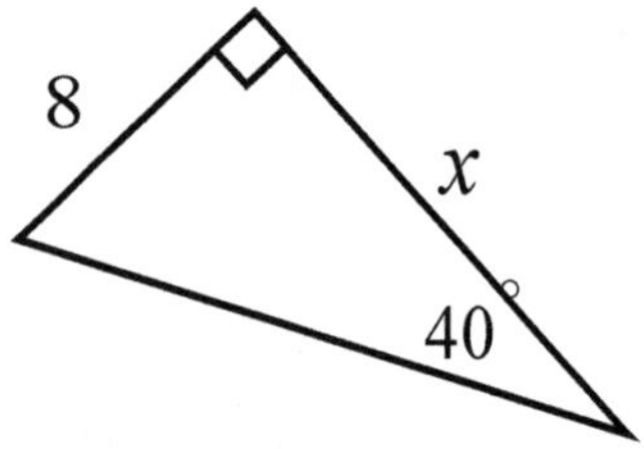

j)

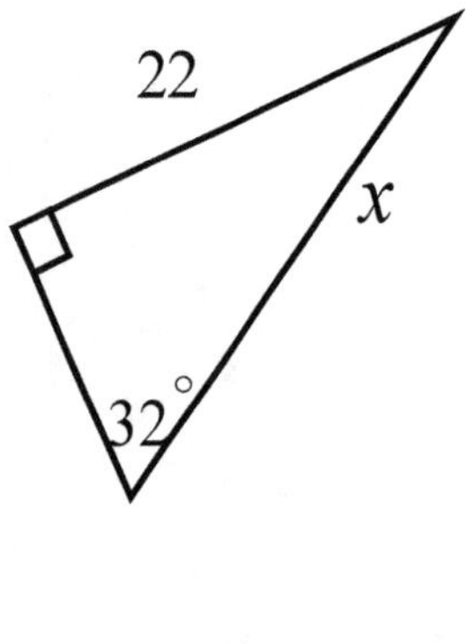

Chapter 10

Finding the Value of Angles

Trigonometry is also useful in finding the value of an unknown angle of a right triangle. This can be done when two side lengths are known. Algebra will again be used for the calculations.

Where Sin, Cos and Tan are used to work out the side of a right triangle, **Inverse Sin, Inverse Cos and Inverse Tan** will be used to work out the angle. On a calculator, inverse sin looks like $\sin^{-1}$, inverse cos looks like $\cos^{-1}$ and inverse tan looks like $\tan^{-1}$. These functions can be accessed by pressing *Shift* sin, *Shift* cos or *Shift* tan, or 2nd *F* sin, 2nd *F* cos or 2nd *F* tan depending on the make and model of the calculator. Note the location of the $\sin^{-1}$, $\cos^{-1}$ and $\tan^{-1}$ functions in the picture below. The S*hift* or 2nd *F* key is usually toward the top left of the keyboard.

E.g. In the triangle below, find the value of θ correct to the nearest degree.

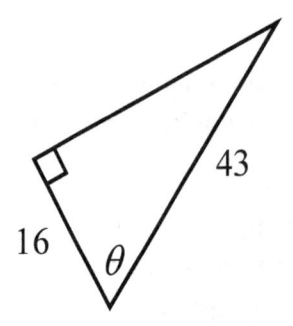

Step 1: Determine which ratio is to be used. (Label the three sides H, O and A)

Since the relevant information is on the Adjacent side and the Hypotenuse, then the Cos ratio is to be used. (SOH CAH TOA)

Step 2: Start with the formula

$$\cos\theta = \frac{A}{H}$$

Step 3: Substitute in the known information. In this case it is the length of the adjacent side, 16 and the length of the Hypotenuse, 43.

$$\cos\theta = \frac{16}{43}$$

Step 4: Make θ the subject. (see Easy Steps Math Algebra).

$$\theta = \cos^{-1}\frac{16}{43}$$

Step 5: Input $\cos^{-1}\dfrac{16}{43}$ into a calculator.

And the answer will be $68°$ to the nearest degree.

Try these questions.

For each of the following, find the value of θ to the nearest degree.

a)

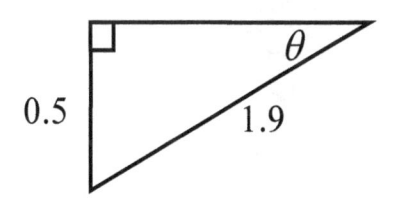

```
      ┌────────────
      │         θ
  0.5 │      1.9
      │
```

b)

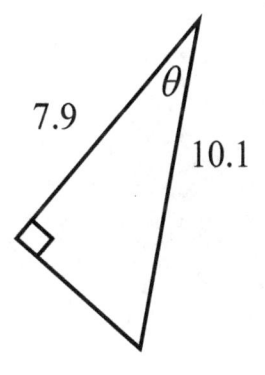

7.9   θ
       10.1

c)

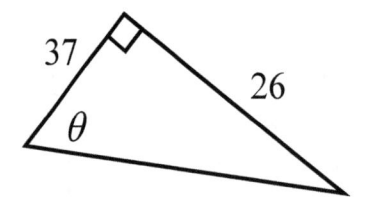

37, 26, θ (right angle between 37 and 26)

d)

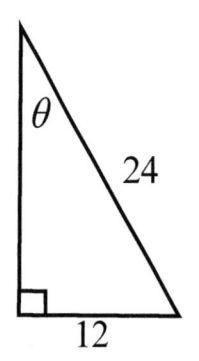

θ, 24, 12 (right angle)

e)

26, θ, 8 (right angle)

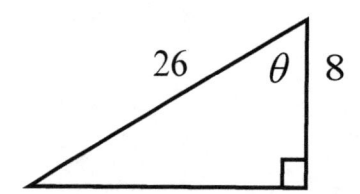

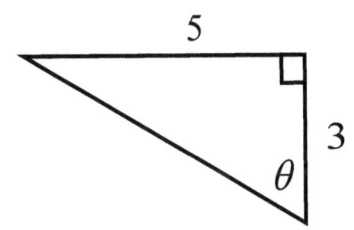

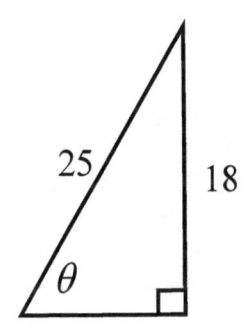

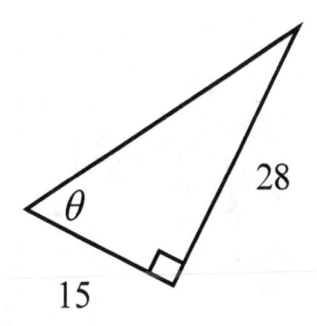

f)

g)

h)

i)

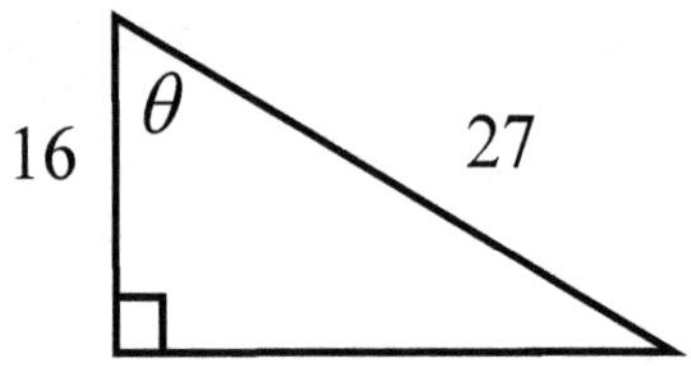

j)

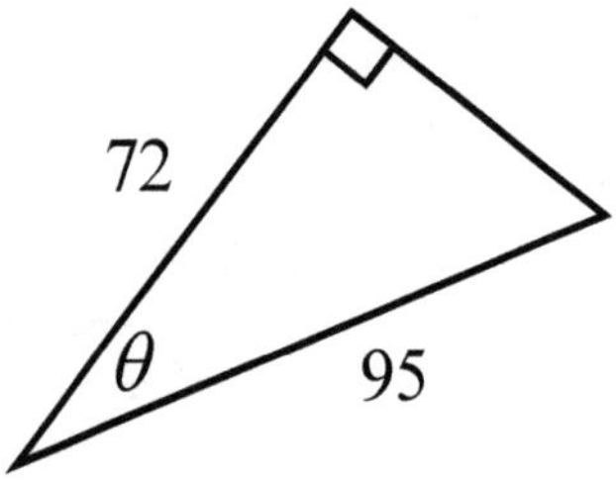

Chapter 11

Angles of Elevation and Depression

In trigonometry the **angle of elevation** refers to the angle from the horizontal upward.

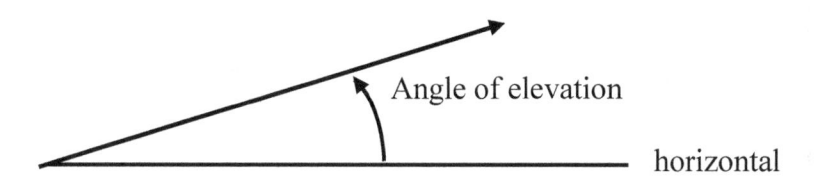

And the **angle of depression** refers to the angle from the horizontal downward.

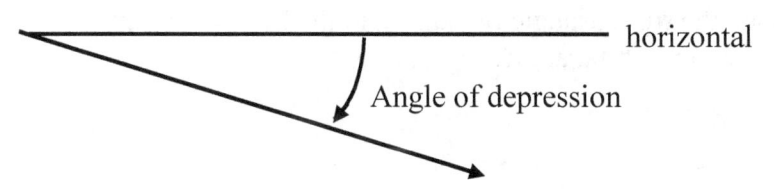

When a question refers to the angle of elevation, or the angle of depression, it is very important to identify the right triangle that can be formed so that the necessary calculations caan be made.

E.g. 1. A person is in a boat 450 meters from a cliff. The cliff is 95meters high. What is the angle of elevation from the boat to the top of the cliff. Give the answer to the nearest degree.

Step 1: Draw out the situation. It does not have to be to scale.

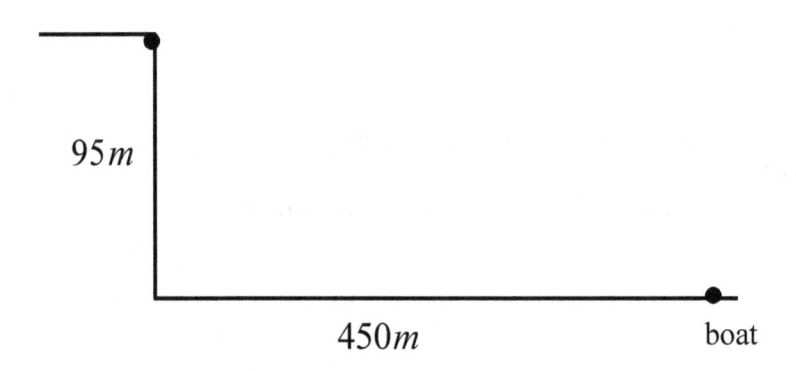

```
        |
   95m  |
        |_____•
              450m                boat
```

Step 2: Create the right triangle by putting in the hypotenuse and identify the position of the angle.

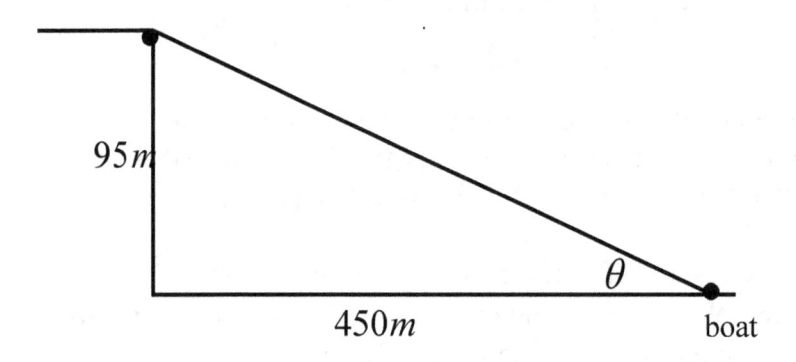

```
        |\
   95m  | \
        |  \
        |   \___θ
        |_____\•
              450m    boat
```

Note the position of the angle. Since the question asked to find the angle of elevation, the required angle is from the horizontal upward.

Step 3: Label the three sides of the triangle with O, A and H and decide which ratio to use.

```
         •
         |\
         | \
         |  \         H
O 95m    |   \
         |    \
         |     \ θ
         |_____\•
           450m
             A
```

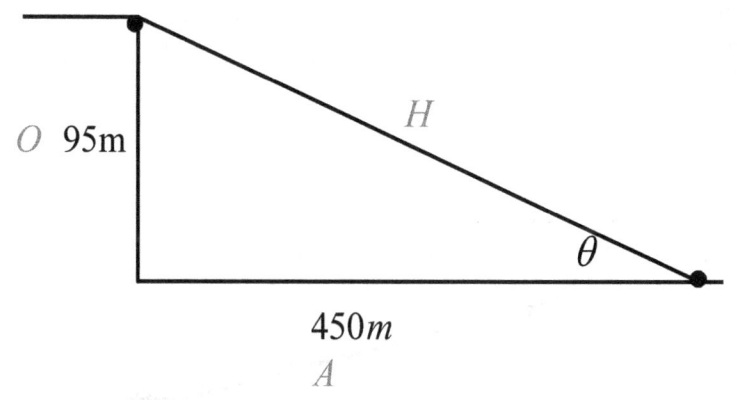

The required information is on the Opposite side and the Adjacent side. Using SOH CAH TOA, the ratio of Tan will be used. (TOA)

Step 4: Start with the formula

$$\tan\theta = \frac{O}{A}$$

Step 5: Substitute in the known information

$$\tan\theta = \frac{95}{450}$$

Step 6: Since the value of angle is to be found, make θ the subject.

$$\theta = \tan^{-1}\frac{95}{450}$$

Step 7: Put $\tan^{-1}\frac{95}{450}$ in the calculator

And the answer will be $12°$ to the nearest degree.

Eg. 2. A forestry officer spots a fire from his tower at an angle of depression of $15°$. The tower is 33m high. How far is the fire from the tower to the nearest meter?

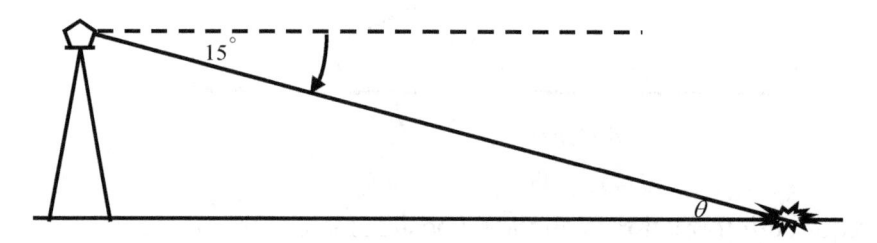

Using geometry of parallel lines, the angle θ is the same as the angle of depression because **alternate angles have the same value.**

This means that in certain circumstances, the angle of elevation equals the angle of depression.

The information from the question and diagram can be transferred to a right triangle.

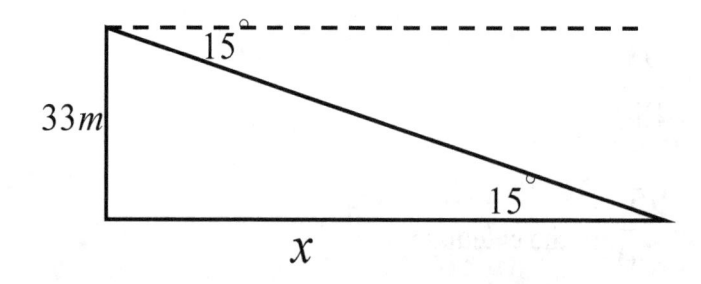

Identifying the required sides indicates that tan is the ratio to be used.

Therefore:

$$tan\theta = \frac{O}{A}$$

$$tan15 = \frac{33}{x}$$

$$x \times tan15 = \frac{33}{x} \times x$$

$$x \times tan15 = 33$$

$$x \times \frac{tan15}{tan15} = \frac{33}{tan15}$$

$$x = \frac{33}{tan15}$$

$$x = 123m$$

Therefore the fire is 123 meters from the tower (worded questions require worded answers).

Chapter 12

Bearings

There are two different ways to express direction using bearings. These are **Conventional Bearings** and **True Bearings.**

Conventional Bearings

Conventional bearings are directions stated as **the number of degrees east or west of north or south.**

E.g. 1.

The bearing N45°E means 45° east of north. As a diagram it would look like this.

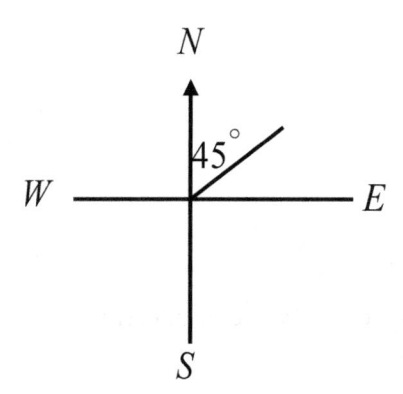

Another way of explaining this is, starting from north, the angle is 45° going in an easterly direction.

E.g. 2.

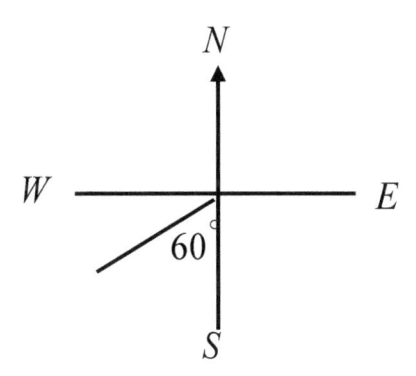

```
        N
        ↑
        |
W ──────┼────── E
       /|
      / |
    60° |
        |
        S
```

This diagram shows that starting from the south the angle is 60° going in a westerly direction, so the bearing would be S60°W

Remember. Start with North or South, indicate the number of degrees, and finish with East or West.

Another way to remember is to divide the compas points into four quadrants.

True Bearings

True bearings give directions as an angles measured **clockwise** from north. True bearings use three digits for the angle and a T is written after the angle to indicate a true bearing.

Using the examples from above.

E.g. 1. The diagram below has a true bearing of $045°T$.

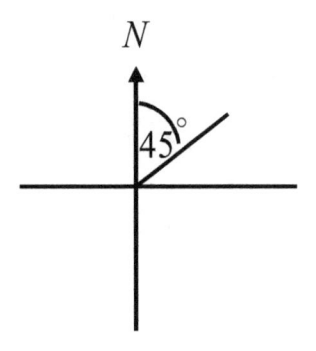

E.g. 2. The diagram below has a true bearing of $240°T$

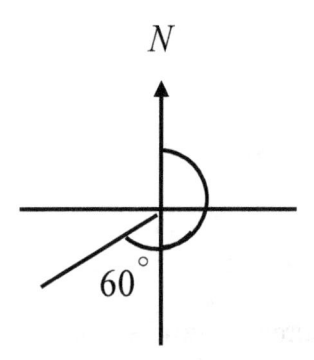

Bearings are useful for practical applications.

E.g. A ship sails 45 km on a bearing of $230°T$. How far south is the ship from its original position.?

Step 1: Start with a diagram of the situation.

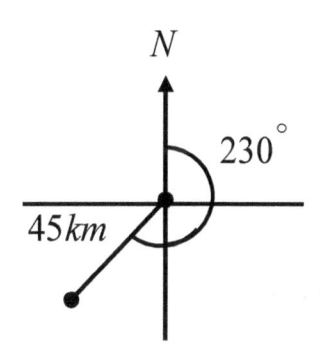

Step 2: Find the right triangle in the situation and label the sides and the angle.

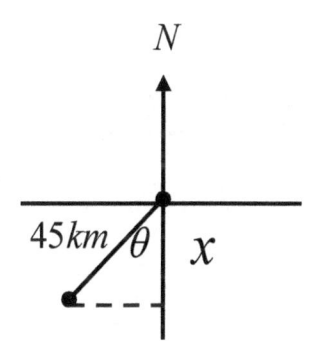

The angle given in the question is 230° and the angle from North to South is 180°, so 230° − 180° = 50°. Therefore θ is 50°.

Transferring this information to a separate right triangle would look like this.

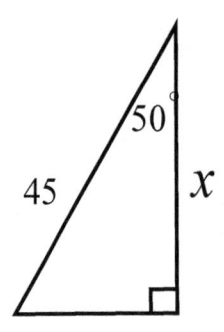

Step 3: Label the sides and decide which ratio to use.

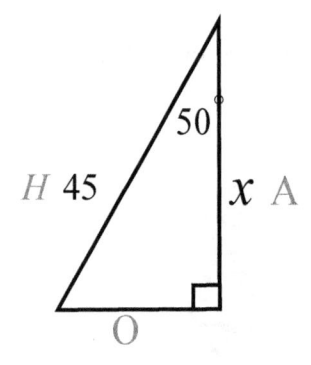

Using SOH CAH TOA, Cos would be used.

Step 4: Start with the formula

$$\cos\theta = \frac{A}{H}$$

Step 5: Substitute in the information available

$$\cos 50 = \frac{x}{45}$$

Step 6: Do some calculations

$$45 \times \cos 50 = \frac{x}{45} \times 45$$

$$45 \times \cos 50 = x$$

Step 7: Use a calculator to work out $45 \times \cos 50$

The answer will be 28.93 km.

Try the following questions.

Write down the conventional bearings and the true bearings of each the following

a)

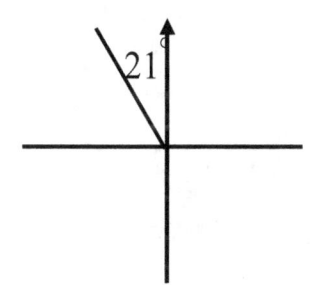

b)

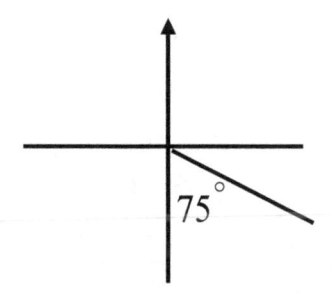

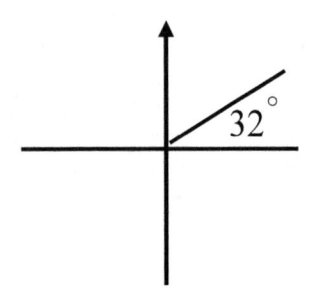

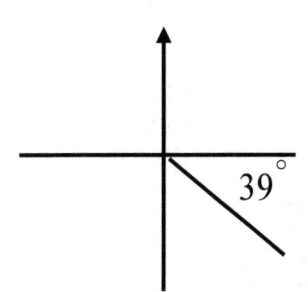

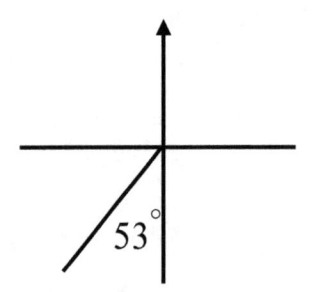

c)

d)

e)

f)

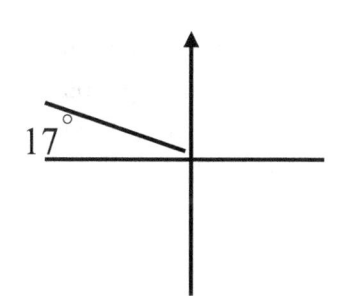

17°

g) A ship sails for 140 km on a bearing of N35°W. How far north of the starting point is it?

h) A helicopter travelling on a true bearing of 100° is now 80 km east of its original position. How far has the helicopter travelled, to the nearest kilometer?

i) A taxi travels 580 m south and then 390 m west. To the nearest degree, what is the true bearing of the taxi from its starting position?

j) An ant walks 22 cm on a bearing of N37°W and then turns NE and walks another 28 cm. How far east is the ant from its stating position?

Note that in some instances, it will be necessary to find values of sides or angles so that other values can be found. Also note that some questions may require a combination of Pythagoras and trigonometry to help find the answer.

E.g. Consider the question below.

A slide in a playground has a vertical support and a ladder as shown in the diagram below. The slide is 2.85 m long and makes an angle os 57° 30' with the vertical support. If the base of the ladder is 80 cm away from the support, find the length of the ladder, to two decimal places (Coffey et al).

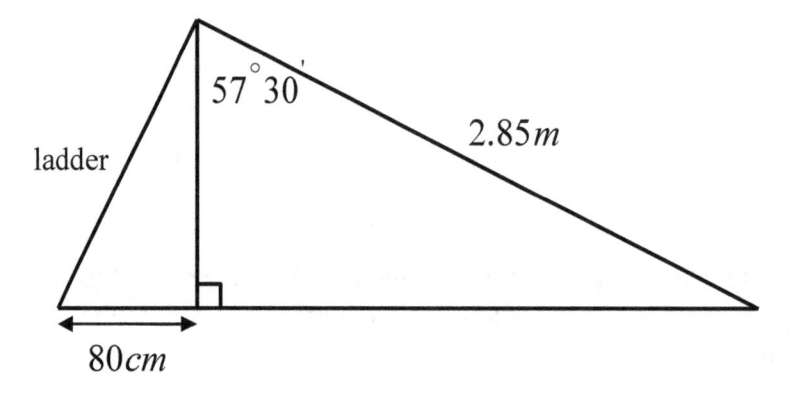

[Diagram: a triangle with "ladder" on the left side, vertical support marked, angle 57° 30' at top, slide labelled 2.85m on the hypotenuse, and base 80cm]

The question is asking for the length of the ladder, but on its own, the left hand triangle does not have enough information to find the answer.

Although the question doesn't ask for it, the height of the support must be found first. This is done by using trigonometry. The support is the adjacent side and the slide is the hypotenuse. Therefore the ratio cos will be used. Label the support x, and the right hand side triangle will look like this;

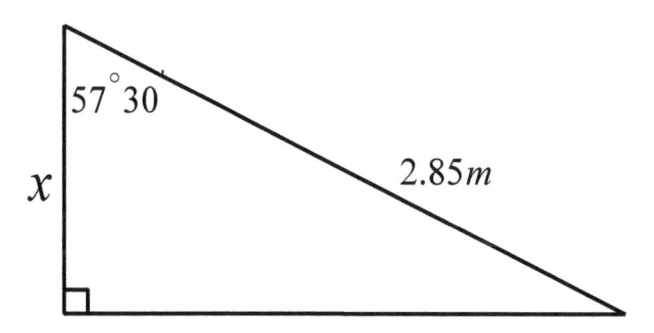

Now do the calculations, starting with the formula.

$$\cos\theta = \frac{A}{H}$$

$$\cos 57°30' = \frac{x}{2.85}$$

$$2.85 \times \cos 57°30' = \frac{x}{2.85} \times 2.85$$

$$2.85 \times \cos 57°30' = x$$

$$x = 1.53$$

So the support is 1.53 m high.

Now the calculations for the left hand side triangle can be completed.

ladder 1.53m

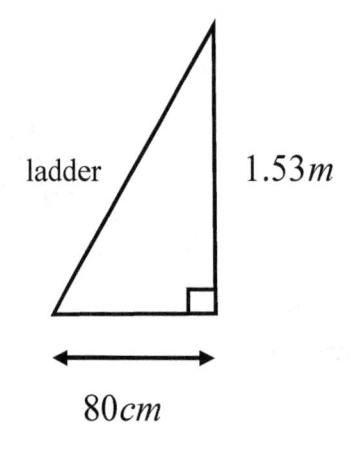

80cm

As there are no angles given for the left hand side triangle, Pythagoras' theorem will need to be used.

The ladder (or hypotenuse) will be **c**. Be aware that the units given above are different. The support is in meters and the base is in centimeters. For the calculations to work, all units must always be the same.

Either use 153 cm and 80 cm **or** 1.53 m and 0.8 m.

Starting with the formula:

$$c^2 = a^2 + b^2$$

$$c^2 = 1.53^2 + 0.8^2$$

$$c^2 = 2.4 + 0.64$$

$$c^2 = 3.04$$

$$c = \sqrt{3.04}$$

$$c = 1.74$$

Therefore the length of the ladder is 1.74 m.

Chapter 13

The Law of Sines (Sine Rule)

There are times when a triangle does not have a right angle at one of its vertices, yet one of the inside angles or a side length still needs to be found. The Law of Sines, or The Sine Rule will work for any triangle <u>where two side lengths and an angle opposite one of these sides is known</u>, **or**, <u>two angles and one opposite side length is known</u>. The rule says:

$$\frac{a}{\sin A} = \frac{b}{\sin B} = \frac{c}{\sin C}$$ to find missing sides

or

$$\frac{\sin A}{a} = \frac{\sin B}{b} = \frac{\sin C}{c}$$ to find missing angles

where a, b, and c are the side lengths of a triangle and A, B, and C are the angles at the vertices.

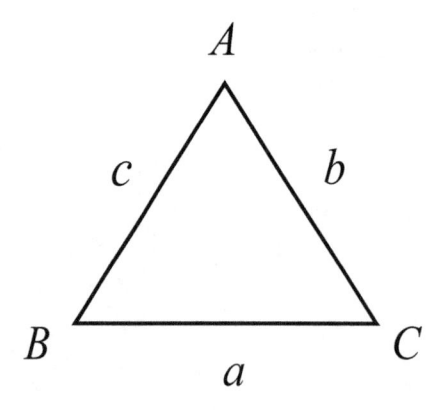

86

In order for the sine rule to work, the labelling of the sides and vertices must be done correctly.
Notice how the lower case letter representing the side is directly opposite the upper case letter representing the angle. This **must** be done for the law of sines to work. See the diagram below.

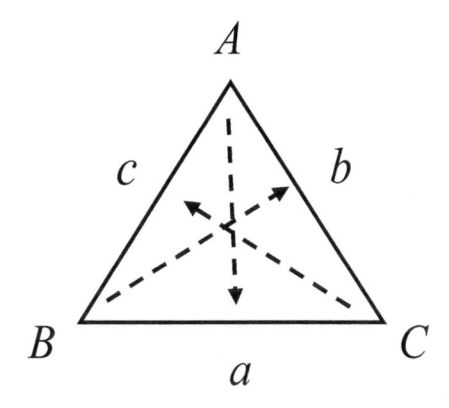

Here is an example.

For the triangle below, find the value of the vertices at A and C and the value of the unknown side.

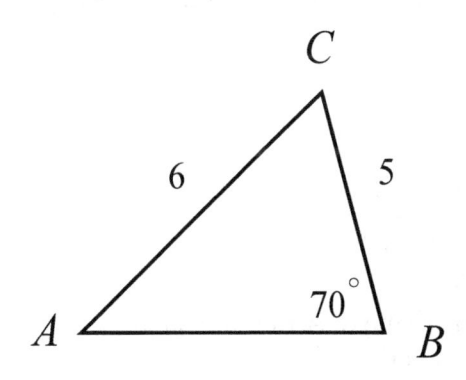

Step 1: Lablel the missing sides and angles of the triangle.

```
        C
    /\
 b 6   5 a
  /  70° \
 A────────B
```

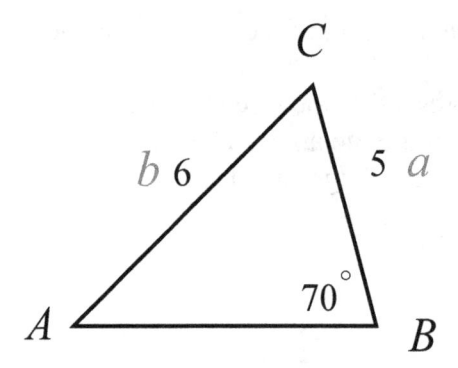

Step 2: Start with the formula (for finding the missing angles)

$$\frac{\sin A}{a} = \frac{\sin B}{b} = \frac{\sin C}{c}$$

Step 3: Substitute in the known values.

$$\frac{\sin A}{5} = \frac{\sin 70}{6} = \frac{\sin C}{c}$$

As there is no information for angle C or side c, this part of the rule can be disregarded at this stage.

So the rule becomes

$$\frac{\sin A}{5} = \frac{\sin 70}{6}$$

Step 4: Do the necessary calculations to make A the subject, as explained in the Finding an Angle chapter

$$\frac{\sin A}{5} \times 5 = \frac{\sin 70}{6} \times 5$$

$$\sin A = \frac{\sin 70}{6} \times 5$$

$$\sin A = 0.7831$$

$$A = \sin^{-1} 0.7831$$

$$A = 51.55°$$

Now there are two known angles in the triangle, $51.55°$ and $20°$. Since the angles in a triangle add up to $180°$ the third angle must be:

$$180° - 20° - 51.55° = 108.45°$$

The triangle now looks like this:

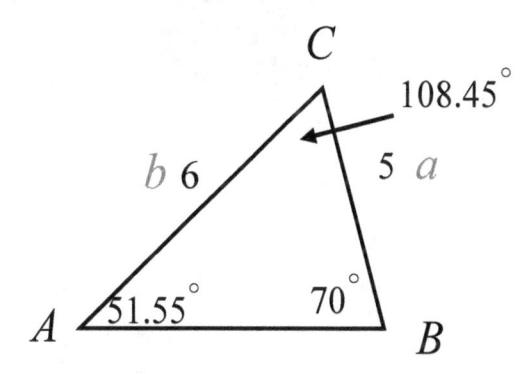

[Triangle with vertex C at top labeled $108.45°$, vertex A at bottom-left labeled $51.55°$, vertex B at bottom-right labeled $70°$, side b = 6, side a = 5]

Now to find the length of side c the original rule would be used again

$$\frac{a}{\sin A} = \frac{b}{\sin B} = \frac{c}{\sin C}$$

Put in the known information

$$\frac{5}{\sin 51.55} = \frac{6}{\sin 70} = \frac{c}{\sin 108.45}$$

Since it is c that needs to be found the part of the rule that is useful is

$$\frac{6}{\sin 70} = \frac{c}{\sin 108.45}$$

Do the necessary calculations to make c the subject

$$\frac{6}{\sin 70} \times \sin 108.45 = \frac{c}{\sin 108.45} \times \sin 108.45$$

$$\frac{6}{\sin 70} \times \sin 108.45 = c$$

$$\frac{6}{\sin 70} \times \sin 108.45 = c$$

$$c = 6.06$$

Chapter 14

The Law of Cosines (Cosine Rule)

The cosine rule is used to find missing sides and angles where the Sine rule does not work, (but try the Sine Rule first).

To find the length of a side, the opposite angle and the other 2 sides are needed and to find an angle, all three sides are needed.

The rule for finding the side length of a triangle, is:

$$a^2 = b^2 + c^2 - 2bc \cos A$$ to find side a, or

$$b^2 = a^2 + c^2 - 2ac \cos B$$ to find side b, or

$$c^2 = a^2 + b^2 - 2ab \cos C$$ to find side c.

The rule for finding an angle inside the triangle is:

$$\cos A = \frac{b^2 + c^2 - a^2}{2bc}$$, to find the angle at A,

$$\cos B = \frac{a^2 + c^2 - b^2}{2ac}$$, to find the angle at B,

$$\cos C = \frac{a^2 + b^2 - c^2}{2ab}$$, to find the angle at C.

Here is an example,

For the triangle below, find the value of the vertices at A and B and the length of side c.

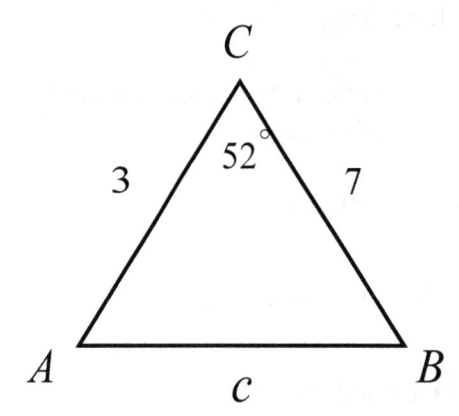

```
       C
      /52°\
   3 /     \ 7
    /       \
   A---------B
        c
```

Step 1: Label the unknown sides of the triangle

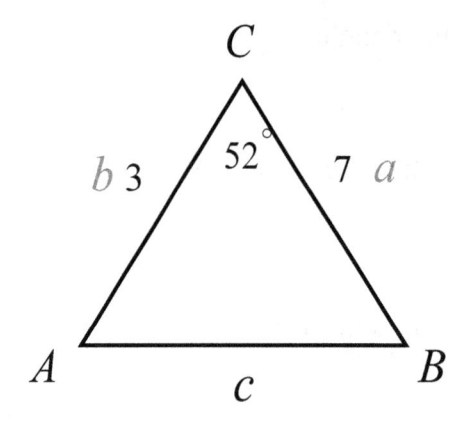

```
       C
      /52°\
 b 3 /     \ 7 a
    /       \
   A---------B
        c
```

Step 2: Decide which version of the cosine rule is to be used. To find the side c, the following rule is the appropriate one.

$$c = \sqrt{a^2 + b^2 - 2ab\cos C}$$

Step 3: Substitute into the rule all the known information

$$c = \sqrt{7^2 + 3^2 - 2 \times 7 \times 3 \times \cos 52}$$

Step 4: Do the necessary calculations to find the value of c.

$$c = \sqrt{49 + 9 - 42 \times \cos 52}$$

$$c = \sqrt{49 + 9 - 25.86}$$

$$c = 5.67$$

To find the angle at vertex A

Step 1: Identify the rule to be used.

$$\cos A = \frac{b^2 + c^2 - a^2}{2bc}$$

Step 2: Substitute in the known information.

$$\cos A = \frac{3^2 + 5.67^2 - 7^2}{2 \times 3 \times 5.67}$$

Step 3: Do the necessary calculations to make A the subject.

$$\cos A = \frac{-7.8511}{34.02}$$

$$\cos A = \frac{-7.8511}{34.02}$$
$$\cos A = -0.2308$$

$$A = \cos^{-1} -0.2308$$

$$A = 103.34°$$

Now that there are two known angles for the triangle, $103.34°$ and $52°$, the third angle at vertex B is:

180°-103.34°-52°=24.66°

Here are some questions to try

Use the sine rule to find the value of variable for each of the following. Angles and lengths are not to scale.

a)

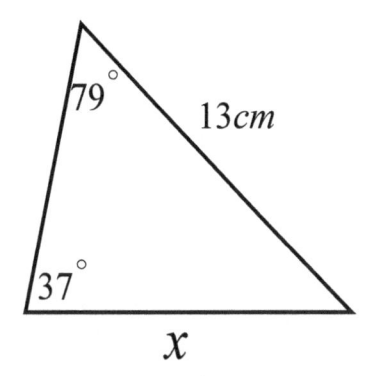

A triangle with angles 79° and 37°, side 13cm opposite the 37° angle, and side x opposite the 79° angle.

b)

A triangle with sides 7cm and 18cm, angle 81° opposite the 18cm side, and angle x opposite the 7cm side.

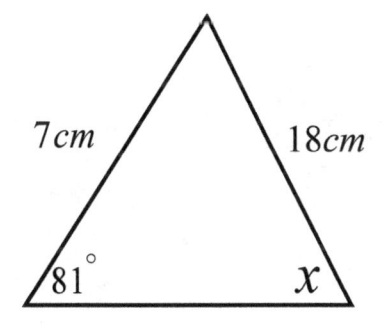

c)

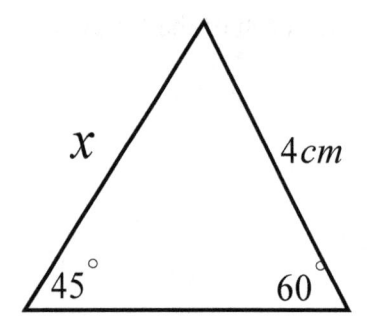

x, 4cm, 45°, 60°

d)

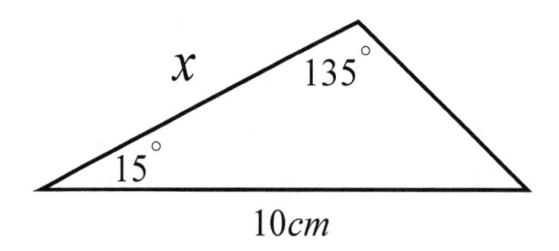

x, 135°, 15°, 10cm

e)

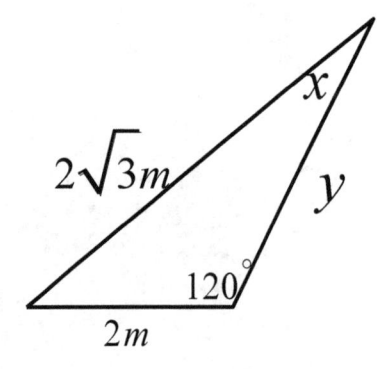

$2\sqrt{3}$m, x, y, 120°, 2m

Use the cosine rule to find the value of the variable for each of the following.

f)

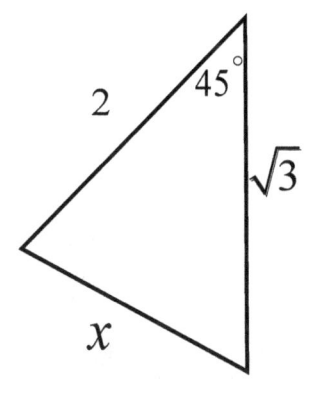

Triangle with sides 2, $\sqrt{3}$, and x, with angle 45° between sides 2 and $\sqrt{3}$.

g)

Triangle with sides 2, $\sqrt{3}$, and x, with angle 135° between sides 2 and $\sqrt{3}$.

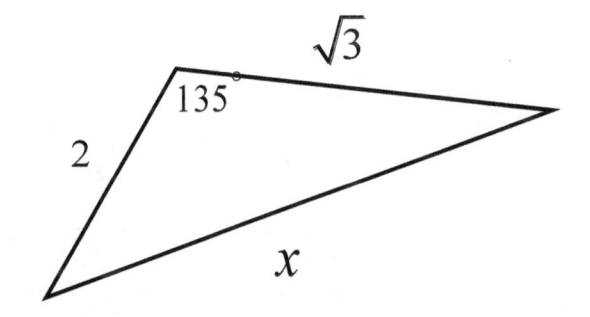

h)

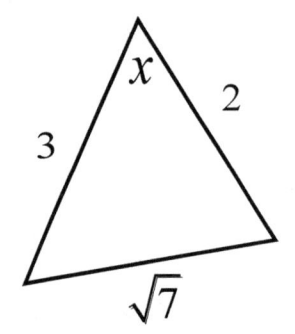

Triangle with sides 3, 2, $\sqrt{7}$ and angle x between sides 3 and 2.

i)

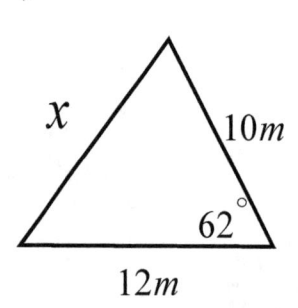

Triangle with side $10m$, side $12m$, included angle $62°$, and angle x opposite.

j)

Triangle with sides $9cm$, $16cm$, $19cm$ and angle x between sides $9cm$ and $19cm$.

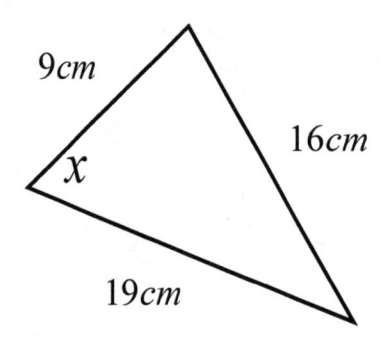

Chapter 15

Mixed Application Questions

Draw a diagram of the situation first then answer the question.

a) A 7 meter flagpole is being supported by two cables, each one 12 meters long. How far apart are the cables fastened to the ground?

b) A ladder is leaning against a wall. The base of the ladder is 3 meters from the wall and it reaches 4 meters up the wall. How long is the ladder?

c) Two steel discs, one with a diameter of 6 cm and the other with a diameter of 8 cm are placed tightly in a square wooden frame. Find the length of one side of this frame.

d) A 6.2 meter tree is casting a shadow along the ground. If the sun has an angle of elevation of 35 degrees, how long is the shadow?

e) A kite is at the end of a long string. It is flying at a height of 28 m from the ground. The string makes an angle of 22 degrees with the vertical. How long is the string?

f) A pilot sees two runway lights in a straight line and at an angle of depression of 20 and 24 degrees. If the plane is 320 m above the runway, how far are the lights from each other?

g) A 5 meter ladder is leaning against a wall. The base of the ladder makes an angle of 65 degrees with the ground. If the ladder slips 85 cm down the wall, what is the new angle the ladder is making with the ground.

h) A road sign is in the shape of an equilateral triangle. Its vertical length is 45 cm. How long are the sides of the triangle?

i) Town A is N29°W of town B and S56°W of town C. If town B is 100 km due south of town C. Calculate the distance between 1) town A and town B and 2) town A and town C.

j) Three towns A, B and C are connected by straight roads. The distance between towns A and B is 25 km and the distance between towns A nd C is 40 km. There is a 20 degree angle between the two roads leading out from town A. What distance is being saved by going directly from town A to town C rather than going via town B?

Multiplication Tables

To make calculations really easy, learn your multiplications tables. Here is a set of multiplication tables from 1 x 1 to 12 x 12 to help you if you need it.

1 x 1 = 1	2 x 1 = 2
1 x 2 = 2	2 x 2 = 4
1 x 3 = 3	2 x 3 = 6
1 x 4 = 4	2 x 4 = 8
1 x 5 = 5	2 x 5 = 10
1 x 6 = 6	2 x 6 = 12
1 x 7 = 7	2 x 7 = 14
1 x 8 = 8	2 x 8 = 16
1 x 9 = 9	2 x 9 = 18
1 x 10 = 10	2 x 10 = 20
1 x 11 = 11	2 x 11 = 22
1 x 12 = 12	2 x 12 = 24

3 x 1 = 3	4 x 1 = 4
3 x 2 = 6	4 x 2 = 8
3 x 3 = 9	4 x 3 = 12
3 x 4 = 12	4 x 4 = 16
3 x 5 = 15	4 x 5 = 20
3 x 6 = 18	4 x 6 = 24
3 x 7 = 21	4 x 7 = 28
3 x 8 = 24	4 x 8 = 32
3 x 9 = 27	4 x 9 = 36
3 x 10 = 30	4 x 10 = 40
3 x 11 = 33	4 x 11 = 44
3 x 12 = 36	4 x 12 = 48

5 x 1 = 5	6 x 1 = 6
5 x 2 = 10	6 x 2 = 12
5 x 3 = 15	6 x 3 = 18
5 x 4 = 20	6 x 4 = 24
5 x 5 = 25	6 x 5 = 30
5 x 6 = 30	6 x 6 = 36
5 x 7 = 35	6 x 7 = 42
5 x 8 = 40	6 x 8 = 48
5 x 9 = 45	6 x 9 = 54
5 x 10 = 50	6 x 10 = 60
5 x 11 = 55	6 x 11 = 66
5 x 12 = 60	6 x 12 = 72

7 x 1 = 7	8 x 1 = 8
7 x 2 = 14	8 x 2 = 16
7 x 3 = 21	8 x 3 = 24
7 x 4 = 28	8 x 4 = 32
7 x 5 = 35	8 x 5 = 40
7 x 6 = 42	8 x 6 = 48
7 x 7 = 49	8 x 7 = 56
7 x 8 = 56	8 x 8 = 64
7 x 9 = 63	8 x 9 = 72
7 x 10 = 70	8 x 10 = 80
7 x 11 = 77	8 x 11 = 88
7 x 12 = 84	8 x 12 = 96

9 x 1 = 9	10 x 1 = 10
9 x 2 = 18	10 x 2 = 20
9 x 3 = 27	10 x 3 = 30
9 x 4 = 35	10 x 4 = 40
9 x 5 = 45	10 x 5 = 50
9 x 6 = 54	10 x 6 = 60
9 x 7 = 63	10 x 7 = 70
9 x 8 = 72	10 x 8 = 80
9 x 9 = 81	10 x 9 = 90
9 x 10 = 90	10 x 10 = 100
9 x 11 = 99	10 x 11 = 110
9 x 12 = 108	10 x 12 = 120

11 x 1 = 11	12 x 1 = 12
11 x 2 = 22	12 x 2 = 24
11 x 3 = 33	12 x 3 = 36
11 x 4 = 44	12 x 4 = 48
11 x 5 = 55	12 x 5 = 60
11 x 6 = 66	12 x 6 = 72
11 x 7 = 77	12 x 7 = 84
11 x 8 = 88	12 x 8 = 96
11 x 9 = 99	12 x 9 = 108
11 x 10 = 110	12 x 10 = 120
11 x 11 = 121	12 x 11 = 132
11 x 12 = 132	12 x 12 = 144

Answers

Surds

a) $4\sqrt{2}$ b) $9\sqrt{3}$ c) $\dfrac{5}{3}$ d) 7 e) $6\sqrt{6}$ f) $\dfrac{\sqrt{2}}{2}$ g) $\dfrac{5\sqrt{2}}{4}$

h) $\dfrac{4-\sqrt{2}}{14}$ i) $\sqrt{15}-\sqrt{10}$

Finding the Unknown Side

a) $c=2\sqrt{5}$ b) $c=10$ c) $c=13$ d) $b=6$ e) $a=12$ f) $c=\sqrt{61}$ g) $a=\sqrt{5.78}$ h) $c=13.04$ i) $a=5.66$ j) $b=3.40$

Identify the Side

a) Opposite b) Adjacent c) Hypotenuse d) Adjacent e) Opposite f) Hypotenuse g) Opposite h) Opposite i) Adjacent j) Opposite

Identify Which Two Sides and Which Ratio

a) $x \& y, \sin\theta = \dfrac{x}{y}$ b) $y \& x, \cos\theta = \dfrac{y}{x}$

c) $y \& x, \tan\theta = \dfrac{y}{x}$ d) $z \& x, \sin\theta = \dfrac{z}{x}$

e) $y \& z, \cos\theta = \dfrac{y}{z}$ f) $\cos\theta (= \dfrac{x}{y})$

g) $Sin\theta(=\frac{y}{x})$ h) $Tan\theta(=\frac{z}{x})$ i) $Tan\theta(=\frac{y}{x})$

j) $Sin\theta(=\frac{z}{y})$

Find the Length of Unknown Side

a) 36.63   b) 33.27   c) 9.18   d) 21.73   e) 7.51   f) 4.04   g) 25.04
h) 13.86   i) 9.53   j) 41.52

Find the Value of θ

a) 15°   b) 39°   c) 35°   d) 30°   e) 72°   f) 59°   g) 46°   h) 62°   i) 54°   j) 41°

Bearings

a) N21°W, 339°T   b) S75°E, 115°T   c) N58°E, 058°T   d) S51°E, 129°T   e) S53°W, 233°T   f) N73°W, 287°T   g) 114.68 km   h) 81 km   i) 214°T   j) 6.56 cm

The Sine Rule

a) 21.20 cm   b) 22.59°   c) 4.90 cm   d) 7.07 cm   e) $x = 30°$, $y = 2$

The Cosine Rule

f) 1.45   g) 3.45   h) 60°   i) 11.46 m   j) 57.05°

Mixed Application Questions

a) 19.5 m   b) 5 m   c) 11.95 cm   d) 8.85 m   e) 30.20 m   f) 160.46 m   g) 47.39   h) 51.96 cm   i) 1) 48.67 km 2) 83.22 km   j) 3.6 km

Glossary of Useful Terms

Surds – A surd is an irrational number written with a root sign ($\sqrt{}$). It is also an exact value compared to it's decimal equivalent which is an approximation. Consider the following:

$\sqrt{2}$ is a surd because it is an irrational number written with a root sign. It's decimal equivalent is 1.4142135… This is an approximation and to use the decimal form it will need to be rounded up or down.

$\sqrt{3}$ is a surd for the same reason.

$\sqrt{4}$ is not a surd because it can be simplified to 2 which is a rational number.

Whenever you multiply a number by itself, the result is a **Perfect Square**. Here is a list of the first twelve numerical perfect squares as well as a couple of algebraic ones.

$1 \times 1 = 1^2 = 1$
$2 \times 2 = 2^2 = 4$
$3 \times 3 = 3^2 = 9$
$4 \times 4 = 4^2 = 16$
$5 \times 5 = 5^2 = 25$
$6 \times 6 = 6^2 = 36$
$7 \times 7 = 7^2 = 49$
$8 \times 8 = 8^2 = 64$
$9 \times 9 = 9^2 = 81$
$10 \times 10 = 10^2 = 100$
$11 \times 11 = 11^2 = 121$
$12 \times 12 = 12^2 = 144$
$x \times x = x^2$

$(x+1) \times (x+1) = (x+1)^2$

The square root of a perfect square is the number that was multiplied by itself.

$\sqrt{1} = 1$
$\sqrt{4} = 2$
$\sqrt{9} = 3$
$\sqrt{16} = 4$
$\sqrt{25} = 5$
$\sqrt{36} = 6$
$\sqrt{49} = 7$
$\sqrt{64} = 8$
$\sqrt{81} = 9$
$\sqrt{100} = 10$
$\sqrt{121} = 11$
$\sqrt{144} = 12$
$\sqrt{x^2} = x$ or $(\sqrt{x})^2 = x$
$\sqrt{(x+1)^2} = (x+1)$

Hypotenuse – the longest side of a triangle (used in Pythagoras' Teorem and trigonometry)

Adjacent Side – the side next to the angle (used in trigonometry).

Opposite Side – the side that is away from the angle (used in trigonometry).

Theta – one of the letters of the Greek alphabet, commonly used to represent the unknown angle in trigonometry. Other symbols are also used

Geometry of Parallel Lines

Parallel lines are lines which are the same distance apart and therefore never meet. They usually have arrowheads to indicate they are parallel.

A line that crosses at least two other lines is called a **transversal.**

Within parallel lines:
Alternate angles are angles that are on alternate sides of the transversal.

Alternate angles are the same, or equal.

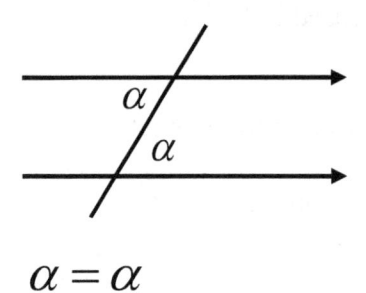

$\alpha = \alpha$

Corresponding angles have positions which correspond with each other, that is they are in the same position, but on the other parallel line.

Corresponding angles are the same, or equal.

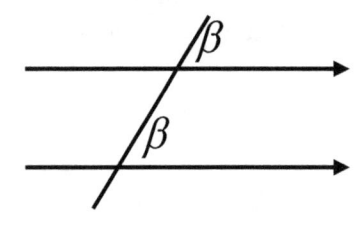

$\beta = \beta$

Co-interior angles are inside the parallel lines and on the same side as the transversal

Co-interior angles add up to $180°$.

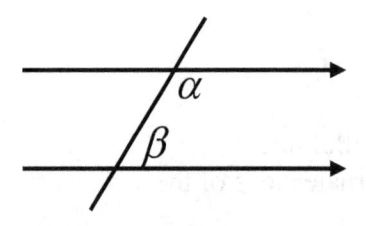

$\alpha + \beta = 180°$

Bearings – a position that is relative to the compass points, North, South, East and West.

Vertices – the corners of a shape or figure. Vertex is the singular version of the word.

Edges – the lines connected to the vertices.

Faces – the surface of the shape.

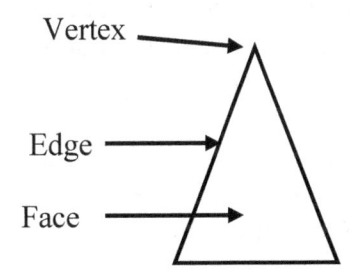

Vertex ⟶ △

Edge ⟶

Face ⟶

Vertical refers to up and down. It is at a right angle to the horizontal.

↕

and horizontal refers to left and right. It is at a right angle to the vertical.

↔

Horizontal can be remembered by thinking about the horizon in the distance. Vertical is the opposite.

Thank You For Reading.

Dear Reader,

I hope you found this **Easy Steps Math – Pythagoras' Theorem and Trigonometry** book useful, either for yourself or for your children.

The **Easy Steps Math** series began as a set of math notes that I used in class for my students to copy from the board. I found that doing this helped the students in at least two ways. Firstly, with their homework, because they didn't forget how to do the work that was explained in class, and secondly, with their results, because they used the notes to study for tests and exams.

Where students in other classes were getting detentions for non-completion of homework, my students were getting homework done, their results were improving and they were enjoying math.

Students from other classes, even older students, were thanking me for my notes, as they were copying them from their peers because they found them so easy to follow and learn from. During a parent/teacher conference, one parent also thanked me because of how his child was able to easily learn the work, and that he, as a teacher, was using my notes in his classes, in his school.

This is when I realised that these notes would benefit many more students if they were published. Thus we are at this point.

I welcome any comments you have about this **Pythagoras' Theorem and Trigonometry** book. Tell me what you liked, loved, or even hated about it. I'd be happy to hear from you. You can email me at robwatchman@gmail.com

Finally, I would like to ask a favour. I would appreciate it if you would write a review of this book so that others can get an idea of how helpful it may be for them or their children. You would be aware that reviews are hard to come by because many readers don't go back to where they purchased their books.

So if you have the time, here is the link to my author's page on Amazon. You can find all of my other books here also: http://amzn.to/1rlW6gr

Thank you so much for reading the **Easy Steps Math – Pythagoras' Theorem and Trigonometry** book and for spending your time with me.

In Gratitude,

Robert Watchman

CPSIA information can be obtained
at www.ICGtesting.com
Printed in the USA
BVHW040222140621
609519BV00014B/901

9 781539 004042